PRAYER IS AN OPEN WINDOW

Elizabeth Rockwood

To
Bill
who has a way of bringing out the highest
and the best in those close to him

Acknowledgments

I would like to express my gratitude to the following for their kind permission to include quotations in this book:

The National Council of the Churches of Christ in the U.S.A. for quotations from the Revised Standard Version of the Bible, copyright 1946, 1952, © 1971 and 1973.

The Westminster Press for quotations from *The Divine-Human Encounter* by Emil Brunner, translated by Amandus W. Loos, copyright 1943.

The Houghton Mifflin Company for quotations from *The Poetic and Dramatic Works of Alfred, Lord Tennyson,* edited by W. J. Rolfe, Student's Cambridge Edition, 1898.

The Macmillan Publishing Co., Inc. for quotations from *The Quest of the Historical Jesus* by Albert Schweitzer, translated by W. Montgomery, 1968; for quotations from *The Cost of Discipleship* by Dietrich Bonhoeffer, translated by R. H. Fuller, 1948; and for quotations from *Letters and Papers from Prison,* revised and enlarged edition, by Dietrich Bonhoeffer, copyright © 1953, 1967, 1971 by SCM Press, Ltd.

The Association Press for quotations from *The Meaning of Prayer* by Harry Emerson Fosdick, Association Press, copyright 1915.

Binford & Mort, Publishers, for quotation from the poem "Proof" from *Kitchen Sonnets* by Ethel Romig Fuller (Oregon: The Metropolitan Press, 1931).

The Princeton University Press for quotation from *Attack upon Christendom* by Sören Kierkegaard, translated by Walter Lowrie, © 1944, 1972.

The Church Pension Fund of The Protestant Episcopal Church in the United States of America for quotations from the following hymns from *The Hymnal of The Protestant Episcopal Church in the United States of America,* 1940: Hymn #21, "O Little Town of Bethlehem" by Phillips Brooks; Hymn #414, "O For A Heart To Praise My God" by Charles Wesley; Hymn #408, "Take My Life and Let It Be" by F. R. Havergal; and Hymn #429 "Day by Day" by St. Richard of Chichester.

Tyndale House, Publishers, for quotation from *Cup of Wonder* by Lloyd John Ogilvie, 1976.

Charles Scribner's Sons for quotation from *The Ordeal of Richard Feverel* by George Meredith, rev. ed. 1921.

The Ave Maria Press for quotation from *Poustinia* by Catherine de Hueck Doherty, © 1975.

The Oxford University Press for quotation from the poem "Prayer" by Hartley Coleridge from *New Poems of Hartley Coleridge,* ed. Earl Leslie Griggs, 1942, used with agreement of the reprint publisher, Greenwood Press, Inc., and for quotation from "Lord of All Hopefulness, Lord of All Joy" by Jan Struther (1901–1953) from *Enlarged Songs of Praise.*

E. P. Dutton for quotations from *The Confessions of St. Augustine,* translated by the Rev. E. B. Pusey. An Everyman's Library Edition. Published in the United States by E. P. Dutton, and reprinted with their permission.

Forward Movement Publications (412 Sycamore St., Cincinnati, Ohio 45202) for the prayer of St. Francis of Assisi and the quotation from St. Patrick's breastplate in *Prayers for All Occasions,* copyright 1964.

Word Books, for quotation from *Prayer and You* by Cecil Osborne, © 1974; for quotation from *Him We Declare* by Cuthbert Bardsley, Bishop of Coventry and William Purcell, Canon of Worcester, © 1968; and Word, Inc., Educational Products Division for "A.C.T.S." method of prayer from *The Edge of Adventure* by Bruce and Hazel Larson and Keith Miller, © 1974.

I would like to express my deepest thanks for the precious gifts of time, encouragement and counsel which I received from the Rt. Rev. Scott Field Bailey, Bishop of West Texas; the Rev. and Mrs. Maurice M. Benitez; Mrs. Lois A. Boyd, Editor of the Trinity University Press; Bill B. Cody, Director of The Laity Lodge Retreat Center; Pat McAlpin; and the Rev. John H. MacNaughton in the preparation of this book.

In addition, I am grateful for the assistance of staff members of the London Library, London, England, who helped this particular descendant of rebel colonists find some sources over there she couldn't locate here. My gratitude also belongs to the Episcopal Theological Seminary of the Southwest in Austin, Texas, and the George Storch Memorial Library at Trinity University in San Antonio for allowing me the wonderful privilege of poring through their fascinating collections of books.

. . . We cannot but speak the things which we have seen and heard.

Acts 4:20

Contents

Introduction

As a little girl, I remember loving to cross a rushing brook near my home. I would plunge my feet up to the ankles in the cold, swiftly moving water and try to find, amidst the sliding rocks of the stream bed, those smooth wide stones which would enable me to reach the far side.

The Lord God, I have found, somewhat to my amazement, loves us—his wobbling, wayward children. Prayer is one of the smooth, wide stones he provides us.

Perhaps you are one of the people who have questions about prayer.

In this little book I would like to explore some of those questions and to share with you how prayer can be as real, as firm, as actual a help as those broad stones were to me when, as a child, I crossed the brook.

1. Does Anything Happen When You Pray?

Does anything happen when you pray?

Recently, with my hands plunged deeply into soapy water, I scrubbed the evening dishes and considered this question. Answers out of my own life and the lives of others crowded my thoughts.

Many years ago, not long before Bill and I were married, I remembered kneeling in my room, wondering how to pray for Bill's mother.

I deeply desired to have a beautiful and loving relationship with her. Yet I barely knew her. I was very young and a little apprehensive of this new kinship, this relative stranger, whose one living child I was about to marry.

How to pray? During the next few days I asked, in my prayers, over and over for guidance in this area.

Finally, these words came to me: "Father in heaven, I pray that our marriage will bring Bill's mother more happiness than she ever thought would come to her."

An optimistic prayer! But she had known some unhappiness and disappointment in her life.

It seemed just right.

So inwardly I prayed those words. Outwardly, throughout the following years, I tried to live in accord with my prayer. Having the usual human predisposition to self-centeredness, I failed often, but always kept trying.

I never told anyone about my prayer. The matter was between me and my Lord.

"Please, Father, may our marriage bring Bill's mother more happiness than she ever thought would come to her." Countless times I offered this prayer for her.

Then came November 26, 1966—our tenth wedding anniversary.

Being the classic example of struggling-young-couple-orbited-by-small-children, we had made modest celebration plans—very modest.

As soon as the three orbiters were caught, fed, and finally contained in crib and beds, we would underscore the date with a quiet evening together and a couple of hot fudge sundaes.

Into this very real and simple scene of children, a sofa that needed recovering, and the fragrance of cooking came an unexpected note from Bill's mother that landed like a missile in my heart and exploded all over with sparks.

Here is her letter, written in response to our anniversary.

My dearest ones:
　　November 26, 1956, was a day that brought me more happiness than I ever thought would come to me.
　　I love you with my whole heart.
Mother

Coincidence? Or does something happen when we pray?

An Episcopal church in Corpus Christi, Texas, planned a weekend dedicated to the spiritual renewal of their congregation. They discovered that mailings, speakers, and meals would cost their parish $1,000.

Feeling sure that the weekend was in God's plan for their church, they wondered how to raise the needed money. They considered many different methods, but none seemed viable.

Finally, they decided to go home and pray about the matter, putting it in God's hands and asking him to help with their problem.

The next day their minister remembered a

"dead" savings fund the church had, its original purpose no longer relevant to the parish. He investigated the amount and found it to be $700. Shortly afterwards the rector received a letter from a former parishioner who had moved with her husband to another city.

She wrote of a recent inheritance which had come to her and, remembering the church with gratitude, she had decided to send a percentage of the amount she had just received.

Her check was for $423—slightly more than the difference needed to attain the required $1,000.

The minister later spoke wonderingly to me of "the extraordinary providence of God."

"For," he said, "connected with the weekend there was an expense we had not forseen, which brought its total cost to precisely $1,123."

Yet the donor had not known about the need of her former church nor the prayers of its parish leaders.

Another coincidence? Or dare we say that he who came to bring us life and that more abundantly does just that? Can we think that he reaches into and touches the common clay of our existence and transfuses it with evidence of his glory?

That he did this in an earlier age is recorded in the Bible. He did not cease to do this when the last chapter of the Bible was written.

Emil Brunner, the Swiss theologian, wrote of the personal and active relationship of God with man, both from the biblical and the current perspective. He used the phrase "personal correspondence" to describe the encounter of the divine Father with the individual.[1]

Several years ago I attended a retreat whose leader, an outstanding author and theologian, impressed me deeply. A few months later, shortly before Christmas, as I was saying my morning prayers, I remembered a special prayer of his: "Here am I, Lord; use me where thou wilt, how thou wilt, with whom thou wilt."

For that day specifically, I made his prayer mine also. Then I set about my tasks. I had a long list of Christmas shopping to complete at a local mall.

As I walked from store to store, I silently lifted up my morning prayer: "Here am I, Lord; use me where thou wilt, how thou wilt, with whom thou wilt."

I had never seen so many people at the mall—swarms, late, as I was, with their holiday shopping. Due to the long waits to be helped and to pay I was not through until after two in the afternoon.

My arms ached with carrying all my packages; the string around one of them bit into my fingers. I waited in a long cafeteria line for lunch.

Juggling tray, packages, and purse, I emerged from the line to find there were no empty tables in the packed restaurant.

I stopped, unsure what to do. Suddenly, just in front of me, two people stood up and left. I dropped into one of the seats. Almost immediately, a young woman whom I had never seen before asked if she could take the other and joined me at the table.

We began to eat in silence, politely not speaking. Then we progressed from passing the salt to conversation about the crowds, shopping, and finally, our children. She was from out of town, I discovered, in for the day to Christmas-shop for her children, who were approximately the ages of mine.

As we began our desserts, I found myself telling her about a program that had brought new life to our church. I went on for some time about this program, telling her of other churches that had tried it and the wonderful new life it had brought to them.

Suddenly I stopped short. She looked stunned, as if I had struck her in the face with a wet rag.

"Uh-oh," I thought. "I don't know her . . . I've gone too far. She didn't want to hear all this."

Embarrassed, I sat in silence while the Christmas crowds and piped carols swirled around us.

She looked at me for what seemed a long time. Then she said, "You won't believe this, but this morning I got on my knees and asked God to lead me this day to someone who could tell me how to bring new life to my church."

Does anything happen when we pray? Not only did we meet—two strangers among hundreds in the mall—but, as a result of our encounter, the particular program I told her about was studied, accepted, and tried in her church with the results she had longed for.

"When I pray, coincidences happen. When I stop praying, coincidences stop happening," said Archbishop Temple. These are words I have found true over and over in my own life.

In the front of a Bible she gave us, my much loved mother-in-law inscribed these words by Alfred, Lord Tennyson:

> More things are wrought by prayer than
>   this world dreams of.[2]

What is prayer? Perhaps of all the definitions of prayer, the simplest, the best, and the most apt is that it is the communion of our spirit with God.

"Communion" can be defined as "sharing." So prayer is a sharing of our spirit with God, a sharing of ourselves with God, a sharing of whatever it is that matters to us with God.

Cecil Osborne writes in his book *Prayer and You*, "Prayer is bringing all of yourself that you can be aware of, into fellowship with all of God that you understand."[3]

For myself, prayer is like opening a window.

I remember once, just after we moved into our present house, coming into the living room late one afternoon. I noticed how dark it had become. Since there was a dutch door, facing approximately west, I unlatched and opened it.

The light flooded in like a dam released— touching, illuminating, brightening, transforming even the darkest corner. The whole aspect of the room was changed.

I remember sitting on the top step to the dining room, looking down into the living room, and wondering at the beauty of it.

And I thought, "This is how it is when we pray: it's like opening a window and asking the Father's light to shine in, to touch, to affect, to transform whatever we hold before him."

Prayer reminds me of the story in the Bible of the woman who thought if she could just touch the hem of Jesus' robe she would be healed. She touched it, and was healed, and in spite of the great crowd pressing around him, he knew about it.

When we pray, we touch the hem of his robe. Because he is the one, living, holy God, this encounter with him can change us and often changes our prayer.

At one time in our lives, Bill went through a difficult period in his business. One day I took the problems this stress was causing me to prayer.

As I lifted my troubles into God's light, he opened my eyes to see that my prayer should be, not for me, nor my anxieties at all, but for Bill.

It is remarkable what God our Father will do with us and our prayers if we come to him. I will always be grateful for the change he wrought that day in me and my prayer.

I began to pray more earnestly for Bill each day. As always happens when we pray for someone, I became aware of him with a new sensitivity. I saw signs of fatigue and strain which I hadn't seen before. I also noticed that he had lost weight. When I inquired about this, he said he hadn't time to leave for lunch so he just ate peanuts and coffee from a vending machine at the office.

As I continued my daily prayers for Bill, I felt an inner conviction that I should fix him a hot lunch each day and take it to him.

I really didn't want to do this. Like so many wives, I had married "for better or for worse . . . but not for lunch."

But the conviction of what I should do persisted. Finally, one day I made the lunch and took it downtown to Bill.

I suppose no hot little meal carried steaming out to a lonely shepherd keeping watch in the craggy hills was ever more warmly received.

After a while Bill's work load lightened and he was able once again to go out at noon.

17

Some months later, in a small group at a church, the question was asked, "When was God most real to you?" My chemical engineer husband amazed me by saying one of the times for him occurred when I had brought him the lunches. He had felt God's strength and comfort in a very real way at that time.

The Lord changes us, and he changes our prayers, that we might become his people, expressing his love and carrying out his purposes, even in the small happenings of our everyday world.

A final illustration of prayer might be found in a magnifying glass. Given sun shining, given paper held in your hand . . . nothing happens, not for a long while anyway. If you stood holding the paper for perhaps a year, it might dry and brown a bit. But, given sun, given paper, and given a magnifying glass interposed between them, the paper will dramatically burst into flame.

I find prayer to be a sort of magnifying glass between the love of God and our prayer concern. Something happens, sometimes something extraordinarily wondrous.

How can our prayer act as a magnifying glass, how touch the hem of his robe, how serve as a window?

"Lord, teach us to pray," the disciples asked (Luke 11:1). As he taught them, so he teaches us.

He accepts us where we are, maybe at a very beginning place, and leads us from there. His answers, like shoes, come in our own sizes.

It is my prayer for you that the following pages serve, in some small way, to bring you— through an increased understanding of prayer— closer to him and to his perfect will for your life.

per p. 108

2. How Do You Hear an Answered Prayer?

"I'd heard about this Man, this Man Jesus," someone said, reflecting on his childhood, "But I didn't know him. It was so much easier to get to know flesh and blood people. I felt I could only really get to know someone I could touch."

But today this same person says, "The most significant thing in my life is my own personal relationship with him."

How did he come to this realization? The change was effected over the years by a gradually increasing awareness of the Presence of God.

First, as a very young man, it was a Presence he felt distantly, a Presence he carefully avoided, whether sensed in others or alone. At one point he began to be aware of him as Someone, sort of far away, who expected something of him. Later, he experienced him as his Forgiver. Finally, he recognized the Man Jesus as being with him everywhere and all the time.

He began to be aware of him in terms of joy. He had all along thought that there was, on the one hand, church and God, in relation to which you were deadly serious, and then there was on the other hand, life, where you could laugh and be yourself.

But he found the reality of the Man Jesus to be One who joyfully loved him, who walked beside him into his living room, through his daily business, out onto the golf course, and was with him still in the dark of night.

How do we perceive him, you and I who mow our lawns and push our grocery carts and count our change?

How do we sense his Presence, how do we have a "hearing" relationship with him?

There are three things to remember in seeking him.

The first is Jesus' own assurance that he is with us always, that he loves and accepts and forgives us; that if we seek him we will surely find him, that, in fact, he even stands at the door and knocks waiting for us to open to him.

The second thing to remember is that we don't need to play a part with him. We need project no image. We can neither shock him nor impress him. We might as well put down our masks before him. He knows all about us.

The third requirement is that we listen.

Suppose you got up one morning and decided that you would not listen to any of the members of your household; you would pay no attention whatsoever to anything they said.

Imagine that you continued your resolve throughout the day, not responding during meals; not looking up if addressed while reading the newspaper; ignoring greetings, confidences, jokes, plans, questions, news, and information. What kind of relationship would you have with your family?

Suppose you continued this for a few days, months, years, a lifetime? What would it do to your relationship with the people around you?

We must listen to God if we are to hear him. He requires from us a silencing of the inward clamor of our own will and plans, and a hearing that is not done in the sense of ears but in the sense of paying attention.

I asked a bright but restless sixth-grade Sunday school class once, "When we talk to God, does he talk back to us?" The room full of twelve-year-old perpetual motions came to a halt long enough to consider the question.

Paper gliders, intended as notes, fluttered and nosedived to the floor; jingling pocket change fell silent; chairs teetering on their back two legs were restored with a clatter to all four.

"Prayer is talking to God," said one at length. Nobody disputed this.

"Yes," I persisted, "but does he talk back to us?"

"Of course not," they concluded, and their perpetual motion resumed.

"He does," I said, "but we don't listen."

But, assuming that we are in fact listening, putting aside our masks and remembering his promises, we will find that the Reality of himself will begin to speak to the reality of ourselves.

We communicate with our children in a variety of ways; with words and attitudes, with examples and actions, appropriate (we hope) to the child and the circumstances.

Our heavenly Father reaches out also to us in many ways. He reveals himself in Christ and through the Holy Spirit, in the Bible and through his church. He speaks to us through the happenings and substance of our everyday lives. He touches us through our feelings and through his creation and through his people.

When he speaks and we hear, his words have the power to change us mightily and to conform us more and more into our true nature, which is in his image and likeness. p. 34

Let me give some examples.

In the seventeenth century, a French footman was looking at a tree, stripped of its leaves for the winter. He contemplated its starkness and considered the change that would come over it in spring, summer, and fall.

He was struck with awe by the wonder of seasonal transformation. As he stood in the cold winter air, looking at the tree and thinking these things, he was overcome by a sense of the power and presence and reality of God as he perceived him through, behind, and at the source of the tree.

He left his position as footman to become a monk, devoting his life with such singular adoration and love that a little book of his letters and conversations is still being reprinted and read throughout the world.[1]

The Lord God, in effect, spoke to Brother Lawrence through a tree.

A young minister was leafing through a magazine when suddenly the faces of some boys on trial for murder in the ghettoes of New York caught his eye. He felt, through the picture, a devastating call by God to leave his position in order to minister to the young people in the slums of New York.

The account of his subsequent work—the hundreds of youth he brought to Christ, pulling them from destructive, potentially fatal drug addictions and lives of crime—has been made into a movie and is the subject material of several books. God spoke to Dave Wilkerson through a pen drawing in a magazine.[2]

These are dramatic examples. But the Lord who created the vast and far-flung universe created also the blade of grass. His words come to us often in quiet, simple, personal ways.

A gentle and sensitive housewife had, one day, to take the family's much loved, but ailing, dog to the veterinarian.

"Poor Fred," she said to him, observing his anxiety as they drove to the vet. "If only you understood that this is going to work for good for you."

But Fred continued to huddle miserably on the car seat. Then she thought how his mind was of a lower order than hers and there was no way he could comprehend.

"You'll just have to trust me, Fred," she said.

It struck her then suddenly, and with clarity, that such exactly was her relationship with her

Creator. She felt at that moment the pull of him, his call to her to relinquish her anxieties and simply to trust in him.

These quiet answers are often heard within the changes wrought by him in our own characters.

I remember the calm and patient attitude of a pretty mother toward her small, active children and her husband who expected an always spotless house and his meals right on time. She had about her at all times, a genuine air of serenity.

"How do you do it?" I asked her.

Her response surprised me for she was someone who had never mentioned her faith to me before.

"Oh," she said, "I'll tell you my secret. Every day I pray for patience. That is my one prayer for myself."

Over and over since then I have found someone's most outstanding and beautiful characteristic to have followed, first, their realization that they had not, nor could not achieve that characteristic on their own; and, second, their prayer for that quality.

"My strength is made perfect in weakness," Paul was told by God (2 Cor. 12:9).

One time a child brought home a disastrously low grade on a report card. His father was grieved and said, "Son, if only you had come to me, I would have been so happy to help you and then this would never have happened."

Our Father in heaven loves us like that. When we take to him our need for his help—to have faith or to be wise or loving or truthful or gentle or strong or forgiving or any good thing, it is his joy to respond.

Then it becomes our joy to perceive his answers taking place in the transformation of our own characters.

Witnessing his strength made perfect in one's own or another's weakness is one of the most beautiful and powerful forms of answered prayer.

There are those of us who experience our most vivid answers to prayer during a crisis.

We tend to go through life riding a raft of our own devising. It may be financial security or popularity or social position or achievement, but then one day our raft falls apart and we cry out to the Father.

I remember a day when a particular raft of mine came apart; it was one of the times I heard an answered prayer.

Bill and I and our three children were living near the Mexican border, where he was an engineer with a large chemical plant. One autumn, he went to Seattle, Washington, as a delegate to a week-long national convention of our church.

While he was gone a tropical storm brewing in the Gulf of Mexico turned into a major hurricane and suddenly headed for our city.

When I heard it was actually coming our way, I turned on the television for further news. In response to the prediction of 200-mile-per-hour winds, the governor was advising everyone who could to evacuate.

What to do? It was almost dark; the roads leading out were not familiar ones to me and ran through literally a hundred miles of barren ranch land. Our only course was to stay.

Our children, ages eight, seven and five, helped me board up the windows. Our backyard was enclosed by a six-foot cedar fence. We lashed the gates shut with ropes and then comtemplated the rabbit hutch, housing mother, father, and eight baby bunnies, all personal friends of the children. We were a little uncertain about just exactly what hurricanes might do to rabbit hutches, but we had some suspicions.

It was our consensus that they all come inside and be established in a bathroom. A six-week-old beagle pupply was another resident of our backyard; he also was assigned a bathroom.

About 11:00 P.M. some thoughtful friends came by and took us and the puppy to their own secure home.

"But not the rabbits," they said.

At 2:00 A.M., as hurricane Beulah roared

through our city, the grandmother of our host family whispered to me, "When the roof goes, throw yourself over the children."

It was a sobering prospect.

However, neither her roof nor ours "went." Others were not so fortunate. Morning found our city ravaged, flooded, and isolated.

Because of highway flooding and wind damage to the airport, we could not be reached by land or airline for days. There were almost no telephones in service. There was neither electricity nor water. There were no incoming supplies of food, milk, or mail. Not only had many homes and businesses and hotels lost their roofs, but entire second floors had blown away or collapsed under the weight of torrential rains. Windows were blown out all over town. Small homes, trailers, and airplanes were found blown into telephone poles, upside down, or caved in. Many streets were either washed away or were under three to five feet of water.

After our friends took us home, the children and I contemplated the situation. The house was wet inside from wind-driven rain, but otherwise undamaged. The six-foot fence was scattered in pieces about the neighborhood. Whole trees were uprooted and flung about our yard in a welter of broken branches and split trunks.

The rabbit hutch was fragmented. Worst of all, we had ten rabbits and the new puppy still in the house . . . with no running water, nor prospect of any, nor even any newspaper or prospect of any!

It was an absolute necessity to get the animals out of the house. But I had no knowledge whatsoever of the kind of carpentry needed to build a fence or reconstruct a hutch. As for chopping up the great broken trees that obscured our yard, I had neither ability nor strength equal to the task.

I could not ask our friends for help. Not only did they have problems similar to mine, but they also had their shattered places of business to look after.

Yet there was no way I could either reach or be reached by Bill. That was when my raft fell apart. Bill had always been *there.* I counted on him totally and absolutely. When there was swift water he was my sure raft. Only now there was swift water and my raft was two thousand miles away.

I went to the Father very simply. I had done all I could or knew to do to care for what he had given me. I had gladly, long before, released Bill in my heart to do the kind of work that had carried him away from me to Seattle.

There was no hesitancy in my mind as I knelt down.

"Father," I prayed, "I need help. Father, I ask you to help me. In Jesus name, Amen."

Somewhere in the back of my numbness and

shock there came a quieting, an assurance, a trust. He was in control.

A few hours later a Volkswagen maneuvered its way in and out of the debris and fallen trees in our driveway up to our house. It stopped, and two tall, strong young men got out. I had never seen them before in my life. They walked directly to me, and, as I stood there amidst the broken branches, I heard an answered prayer.

"Lady," one of them said, "do you need help?"

For two days they worked, putting up the fence, rebuilding the hutch and finally, getting the animals out of the house. After that they sawed and stacked the shattered trees, piling up heaps of brush and branches into a mini-mountain at the edge of the lawn.

They wanted no pay. They said they had driven to our city just before the roads were closed, from the University of Texas, some three hundred and fifty miles away. They had thought that perhaps they might be able to help someone.

I never saw them before then, and I have never seen them since.

How do you hear an answered prayer?

You hear it in trees, in pictures, in animals, in the transformation of a character—in countless ways—if you listen, and in words like these:

"Lady, do you need help?"

31

3. Be Thou Lord of My Life . . . Except . . .

There is a lovely community we visited, nestled in a valley of the Adirondack mountains. One of its charms is a great, clear stream, flowing down from a mountain top, full of lively fish. The waters wind, with a joyful, noisy commotion, through the fields and woods.

One summer, however, this stream, so prized and enjoyed, began to dwindle. The water level on the banks dropped. The fish died. The song of it fell to a whisper.

Investigation above the stream revealed the work of beavers. They had managed to engineer an extraordinarily successful dam.

Because the community in the valley is dedicated to the protection of wildlife, a debate set in among local citizens as to how they might save their stream without harming the furry engineers.

Finally a plan was devised for catching the beavers and transporting them to another location. Subsequently, the people of the community cleared away the rubble and the water flowed singing once again down into the valley.

We tend, as we go through life, often without intention, to allow such dams to accumulate between ourselves and God. Until we become aware of them, are sorry and ask his forgiveness in prayer, we deny ourselves the free flow of his Spirit.

A friend once told me of an experience she had while deer-hunting on a West Texas ranch. It was, at that time, legal to kill a buck but not a doe. By mistake, alone in the woods, she shot and killed a doe. Realizing her error, she left the animal and returned to the ranch house. Her friend, who owned the ranch, inquired about her day. "Oh," she found herself saying, "I didn't kill any deer."

She suffered guilt over this for many years afterward. Finally, confessing her falsehood to God and to her friend, she felt relieved, purer in heart and closer to God.

There is a great peace, a cleansing that comes

with repentance, the prayer of confession and amendment of life.

My friend's transgression was a small one. But the wonderful thing is that the same principle applies to great stumbles as well as small ones.

Have you ever missed a turn on the highway? Maybe you went quite a long way in the wrong direction before realizing your mistake. But we can't go too far when we do this. Somewhere, at last, when we recognize our error, we can turn around. The right road will still be there.

The prayer of confession is always open to us. We can start again. We are promised "abundant pardon."

The times we turn away from God remind me of laundry. When we have a pile of laundry, we don't just stand and stare at it—all the socks and shirts and towels heaped up. And we don't pretend it's not there, and walk away from it.

We wash it.

It is the same with our transgressions. There is no good in standing, staring at them, hating ourselves. And it's no good to pretend they are not there. But we can take them to our heavenly Father, confess them, and be washed in his light.

I would like to say something now about people who have no debris between themselves and God.

We have a much loved friend who, at one point in her life, experienced a remarkable dilemma. She worked hard and earnestly for many worthwhile causes.

She visited the sick, the elderly, and the shut-ins. She baked cookies and took them to everyone from Cub Scouts to newcomers in her parish. She taught Sunday school. She served on the committees of her church. She served in community organizations. Also, at no small sacrifice of her time and strength, she served as chairperson of various worthy causes in her community when called upon to do so.

She thought it strange that, after all her good works, she had an empty feeling. She also found that she could not join in prayers of confession. She had, after all, nothing to confess. Could any woman be doing more than she?

One day, during a church service, the words "Jesus Christ came to save sinners" struck her. "But," she countered silently, "if Jesus Christ came to save sinners, what has he to do with me?"

Immediately she prayed to know if she had any sins. And immediately the answer came. Her deeds were being done in the main part for the admiration, praise, and approval of others.

From that realization came repentance and release from what had amounted to an almost blind compulsion to busy good works. There came a deeper, truer relationship with Christ and a freedom to be his person as he quietly showed her the way.

I remember a precious little lady, with red

hair piled on top her head, who once spoke on this subject. I never knew her name, but I hope I'll always remember her words.

"I clearly had no faults," she said, "but I asked God to reveal them to me if I had happened to overlook anything. He did. They came, one by one, like logs surfacing to my attention."

One in particular that she told about was her relationship with her husband. She came to see that it was a selfish one in which her main objective was never to do more than "her share."

She confessed her self-centered approach to this relationship and began to treat her husband "as if he were the Lord."

Her first effort in this direction took place during a television commercial. They had an unspoken rule that she got the drinks and snacks during the first advertisement. He was then to replenish the snacks during the second. This time, when it was his turn, she got up first, put her hand on his shoulder and said gently, "No, honey, you rest. Let me do it."

She didn't find this new way of relating to her husband easy. "But after a while," she said, "he began treating me in the same way."

And then this upright little lady's voice dropped to a whisper, and tears filled her eyes as she said, "And our life became a heaven on earth."

I remember someone saying once, "But that's

scary. I wouldn't want to know what my faults are."

The best answer to her that I know is found in a story told me by one of the Sisters of Mary.[1]

She said one year her order of Sisters conducted a weekend women's retreat which had an unusual feature. In the main room of the retreat house there was a treasure chest.

The Sisters never referred to it, but the women kept glancing at it. Finally, one of them could stand it no longer. "What is that for?" she asked, pointing. "What is in that chest?"

"Ah," said one of the Sisters, "inside the chest is the secret of joy; no matter what your age, no matter where you are, no matter what your circumstance."

But the Sisters would say no more about it. Throughout the weekend the curiosity of the women concerning the treasure chest began to reach painful proportions.

Finally, on the closing day of the retreat, a Sister carrying a key came in and headed for the chest. The women flocked after her; then, as the Sister turned the key and opened the lid, they sighed and looked at one another with disappointment.

Inside, lying on the bottom, was a slim pamphlet written by one of the founders of their order. It was titled "Repentance, The Joy-filled Life."

Repentance? The secret of joy, no matter what your age, no matter where you are, no matter what your circumstance? How can this be?

Albert Schweitzer once wrote, "Jesus means something to our world because a mighty spiritual force streams from him and flows through our time also. . . . It is the solid foundation of Christianity."[2]

Our prayerful repentance for the points of resistance we have in our lives to the will of God opens us to the free flow of that Spirit and always, unfailingly, leads us to joy.

When I look back on my own life, I can see how I went to God in the beginning saying, "Be thou Lord of my life . . . except for these . . ."

And it was as if I withheld from him a handful of pebbles, precious to me. And it has been as if, bit by bit, as I am able, he has called me to surrender the pebbles one by one. It has not been easy, but always afterwards I have been so glad, so very glad that I did.

An example of this took place when I was nineteen. I was walking on the beach trying to decide whom to marry. There were several adorable possibilities. As I prayed for guidance in this matter there came to me the thought that perhaps God did not want me to marry any of these young men . . . that perhaps—even more unwelcome thought—he did not want me to marry anyone at all.

My prize pebble was being called for. Its name was "My Will for My Life." And "My Will for My Life" was to marry and have a happy home with someone.

It was with a great inner struggle and wrench that I went to a little church near the beach and there, in the cool and silence, gave up to God my most precious pebble.

I expressed in prayer my willingness never to marry, if that was his will, and asked only, simply, that he show me his will for me.

There came a wonderful peace and freedom in my heart following the prayer.

Later, when I first met Bill, we were both given, almost immediately, an inner and absolute conviction that our marriage was part of God's plan for our lives.

Nearly twenty years after our wedding, a new minister at our church observed, "Betse, you and Bill have such a beautiful marriage. There's a perfect balance between your personalities."

That was not my doing, nor Bill's. It was a gift.

It is as if for every pebble we ever give up to God, he will give back to us a jewel in its place.

. . . They cleared away the . . . rubble and the water flowed singing once again down into the valley.

4. Has Prayer Ever Changed Anything in Your Life?

Has prayer ever changed anything in your life? Has it had any effect on your circumstances? Could you say that anything in your experience has been altered because of prayer?

A few years ago, following some unusual stress, a dear friend of ours collapsed with a nervous breakdown. Hospitalization, counseling, and electric shock were required to bring her back to a world that had proved too difficult. Yet, after she returned home, she found her recovery was still incomplete. She felt shattered and painfully unsure of herself. It was hard for her to make a decision. She distrusted her ability to cope with such simple tasks as going to the market.

As she sought to put back together the pieces of her being, she sensed that part of her healing must involve reaching out once again into the world.

Prior to her breakdown she had been an active church member. Yet now something in her resisted her former commitment. Was not life hard enough, she wondered, without the further complication of religion?

It was at this point that she met with a bishop of her church, a man known and respected by many for his gentle and Christlike character.

"It was not so much anything he said," she later told me, "but a quality within him, a sort of indescribable Holy Absolute, which pursued me in my heart after I left him and drew me, irresistibly back to God."

She then began to pray for a useful work to do, something that would be of benefit to others. It came to her one day, while reading a newsletter concerning a large, nearby retirement community that perhaps she could answer a request mentioned in it for volunteers. She felt a strong inner conviction that this was God's answer to her prayer.

Shortly thereafter, she began to work with the residents of the community. She found that her recent experience of illness had left her with just the qualities of compassion and understanding to reach some of the elderly patients who were having problems. Comprehending their feelings, she was able to gently help them out of their depression and withdrawal from life. As she ministered to their needs, she herself gained in strength and effectiveness.

Her initial prayer for useful work had been abundantly answered. But there was more.

After several years of dedicated volunteer service she was elected the first woman chairperson of the board of the retirement community.

Aware of the many problems confronting the board, and sensing her own inability to solve them, she continued to turn to prayer. She, in fact, wrote a prayer in letter form and propped it up on her desk, a daily reminder of the source of her strength.

This is what she wrote:

Dear Jesus,
Please be Chairman of the Board . . . through me.

Had her prayer any measurable results? Did, in any way, the life of Christ flow through her and affect her work in some visible way?

The community was owned and run by several Protestant denominations. During her tenure as chairman there came a new, very evident harmony between the representative members of the ecumenical board. Further, she was, literally, led through prayer to offer the job of chief executive officer of the community to a man with outstanding qualifications who had formerly refused the job. He accepted. In addition, as the community flourished under her leadership, an anonymous donor was inspired to make an unprecedented gift to it for the amount of one million dollars. With these unexpected new funds the community expanded with forty more apartments for those she fondly called her "senior saints."

Finally, because of the exceptional programs and high standard of care, shortly after she completed her two years in office, a major television network presented a thirty-minute nationwide documentary on the community.

Why the success? How could such productivity pour forth from one who had been so very broken? If you were to ask her, she would point you away from herself and back to the prayer propped up on her desk.

"Our Lord can use us best in our inadequacy," she told me recently. "It is not self-sufficiency but God-sufficiency that counts. When I look back," she said, "I know it was he who opened all the doors, put all the right words in my heart, and gave me all the wisdom I needed."

The prayer of petition, the prayer of asking, brings us into the flow of his life.

"Give us this day our daily bread," Jesus taught us to pray—bread for our bodies, souls, and minds.

As we pray each day the form of bread we require may vary. "Give me this day the grace to follow you, Lord," might be our prayer, or, "Give me this day a friend in my loneliness." Maybe our need is "hope in my despair, Lord" . . . "comfort in my grief" . . . "trust in my fear." Perhaps we join the ancient plea, "Lord, I believe. Help thou my unbelief." There are those who have prayed, "Give me this day a job, Lord," or "Shelter, Lord. My family needs a house."

Several years ago Bill and I were planning to move to another city. After many years as an engineer with a large corporation he had purchased his own business in the city where he had been born. We had always wanted to bring up our children there. The move was the fulfillment of a long time dream.

Our only problem had to do with housing. That is, my only problem had to do with housing. For Bill, there was no problem.

"What we do," said Bill absently, his mind mainly absorbed by the pressing business challenge before him, "is rent an apartment. After we've become more familiar with the school districts, residential areas, and so forth, then we can proceed slowly and thoughtfully to look for a house to buy."

I couldn't disagree with the soundness of his position. He was absolutely right. I was thrown into that lonely land mothers can occupy when their instincts are in conflict with logic.

The move, though we confidently anticipated it would work for the children's good in the long run, was, at present, costing them their friends and the only home any of them could remember. Tears had been shed. In fact, their howls of protest had all but rent the ceiling.

I was concerned that an apartment would heap yet further misery by denying our seven-, nine- and ten-year-olds the freedom of movement and outdoor activities that had always been a joyful part of their home existence. Worse, an apartment could well mean the loss of their pets; a disreputable beagle and an ancient rabbit, with whom they communicated, slept and romped interchangeably.

It occurred to me that a compromise might be found in a rent house. Bill agreed, as long as it didn't cost more than an apartment. The real estate agents, however, were discouraging.

"There's really not much available," they advised us by long-distance phone.

I can only pray for something when I feel, to the best of my understanding, that my request is both in line with God's will and that I am doing, for my part, all that I can.

In this instance, I had no doubt that the Father desired to care for us. I had long ago taken Jesus' promises concerning the "lilies of the field" (Matt. 6:28–30) to heart. And I was willing, on my side, to write letters, make phone calls, walk, look, ask—all that was necessary to find a house. This I began to do. But I needed God's help.

I prayed earnestly, not only for a house to rent but, specifically, for a house with a fine, big yard.

A few days later I went to our new city and began sifting through the available houses with a real estate agent. At the conclusion of our first day of looking, as the afternoon shadows drew out across the lawns of a quiet neighborhood, she pulled up before a house which had recently come up for rent.

It had sufficient bedrooms for us, a satisfactory kitchen and a living room with a delightful stone fireplace. But its most outstanding feature was its enormous and beautiful yard. Sweeping from back to front, it was substantially larger than the one we had.

There was a low stone wall in the backyard with tiny red roses tumbling over it and wonderful big trees for climbing, swings, and shade. The rent, incredibly, was exactly the limit Bill had given me for an apartment.

But there was more, for this house was

touched with a blessing of such tenderness that I am convinced it could have come only from the Father's hand.

Out of a city containing approximately one million people, the large and lovely backyard faced, across a quiet street, the front yard of the children's godparents.

There is a hymn whose words, because of their simple truth, come often to my mind.

> Oh, what peace we often forfeit,
>   Oh, what needless pain we bear,
> All because we do not carry
>   Everything to God in prayer.[1]

We sometimes forget this truth. Other times it may appear simplistic to us. Or, perhaps we question whether our particular need could really be of any interest to Almighty God.

"Anyway," we might rationalize, "I'm getting along okay without his help."

Such attitudes cause us to lose out on so many of the beautiful gifts our Lord desires to give us through the opening of our hearts and lives in trust to him—gifts not only for our physical needs, but for our emotional and spiritual needs as well.

A long-time bachelor friend of ours was facing a difficult business day.

"I just dreaded it," he later told me. So he

turned it over to the Father. "Help me through it, Lord," he prayed, before going to work.

That morning his nephew was unexpectedly moved to call him at his office and invite him for lunch. The warmth of the invitation and the prospect of his relative's companionship cheered him through the morning.

In the afternoon, a friend called, also spontaneously, to invite him for dinner that night. He was upheld once again, this time by the prospect of the friendship awaiting him at the day's conclusion.

By night, his morning prayer of asking had become an evening prayer of gratitude.

Our prayers of petition, whether for great things or small, fling open the windows of our beings that our needs might be met by the Father.

I remember, when I was very young, being often inwardly rebellious, negative, and angry. I learned, of necessity, to control the expression of these feelings, but they continued to storm within me.

As I came into my teenage years, I kept reading in the Bible about the peace of God— peace inwardly in one's heart and outwardly in one's relation to the world. I longed for this peace and felt that, somehow, I was missing the mark of what God wanted for me by not having it. But, after repeatedly trying and failing, I found I could in no way manufacture inner peace.

At first I was puzzled. But then I understood.

I began, humbly, to go to the Father in prayer, asking for this particular kind of bread, this gift of his peace which I could not achieve on my own. I persisted in this prayer over a period of years.

Gradually my hostilities melted away and were replaced by a peace so sweet that I stumble for words to express it. It was a peace that had nothing to do with circumstances. There came an inward gentleness, a quiet which, from time to time to this day, deepens into an overwhelming awareness of the beauty and love of God.

After awhile the change which took place in me inwardly began to become evident outwardly.

When I was married, one of my bridesmaids commented, "You're bound to have a happy marriage, since you never argue. In fact," she laughed, "I'll let you in on a secret. I've even tried to make you mad but I never could."

A few years later a friend, with whom I had been doing some church work, suddenly observed, "You have a peace about you."

More recently, another friend burst out with, "What do you go around being so peaceful for all the time?"

My friends were observing no achievement of character, no natural tendency. They were glimpsing a gift, a fragment of the Father's Kingdom, shining in a part of a person where there had been only darkness before.

These gifts of his come like our presents to

our children, in all shapes and sizes and suited to the recipient. Further, they can be touched with a sort of life and glory of the Father which we can neither comprehend nor explain.

A close friend, a beautiful and accomplished young woman, always an outstanding leader in her community, realized, in her late thirties, that her dedication to Christ was incomplete. She then committed herself to him on a deeper level, asking him to be Lord of more of her life.

Almost immediately she became aware that, although she had many friends, her relationships with them were cursory. Outside of her family, she didn't really care deeply about other people.

She asked the Lord in prayer for the grace to care about her friends.

Sometime later she received a call informing her that a former schoolmate, who lived quite far away and whom she only occasionally saw, had cancer of the bone marrow.

She was struck to the heart by her friend's situation. As she put down the receiver, tears began streaming down her cheeks. She could not stop the tears and, finally, telephoned a member of her prayer group.

"Something's the matter with me," she said. "I've received this news and I can't stop crying."

"Don't you remember your prayer to care

more for others?" came the response through the phone. "It looks like it's being answered."

A few days later my friend began regularly to attend healing services at her downtown Episcopal church on behalf of her striken schoolmate. She also called, wrote, and, finally, despite the distance, went to visit her.

After her visit, the sick young woman, whose weight had dropped to ninety-eight pounds, who was bedridden, in excruciating pain and given but a few weeks to live by her doctors, began to show a marked improvement.

Her fever dropped to normal. Soon she got up and began to walk, first with a cane and, later, without it. She drove her car again, then progressed to taking trips with her husband. Two years later she was going to parties and traveled a thousand miles across the country to visit her son in college.

In explanation of her improvement, she told my friend, "When you came to me, with your hand outstretched in friendship and love, there was something in you that gave me the will to live."

My friend's prayer to care had results far beyond any she could have known to ask for.

"All who call on God," wrote Martin Luther, "in true faith, earnestly from the heart, will certainly be heard, and will receive what they have asked and desired, although not in the hour or in the measure, or the very thing which they ask; yet they will obtain something greater and more glorious than they had dared to ask."[2]

It is an ever-unfolding wonder to me how the Father's gifts come to us imaginatively, unexpectedly, and precisely where we are. They fall like snowflakes from the Creator's hand, infinite in variety, exquisite in conception.

There is no real need we cannot take to him. There will be an answer, though not always the one we expect.

When I was still in my twenties I had to preside over a potentially difficult meeting in which opposing points of view would be represented. Most of those who would be present were more mature than I. I keenly felt the gap caused by my youth and inexperience.

The morning before the meeting I spent some time on my knees before leaving home. I felt guided to pray in a way I never had before.

"Father," I asked, "please, for this one day, may others respond not to me at all, but to your holy Son as he lives in me."

Strengthened, I went to the meeting. It proceeded better than I could have hoped. A quiet and surprising harmony maintained among us, and our meeting was concluded peacefully and fruitfully.

Afterwards, feeling thankful, I headed for my

car. My way led through a kindergarten playground. I had often crossed it while the little students played. I didn't know that year's crop of preschoolers, so there had never been any communication between us.

But this day was different. As I came by, several of the children stopped their play, broke away from the others and ran to me. They took my hands in their little fingers and drew me over to a bench under a shady tree. They climbed onto my lap, wrapped their arms about me and looked into my face. Incredulous, I was too dazzled with pleasure to know what to say. There, under the tree, with shining eyes, they confided the things that were important to them. Overcome with delight, touched to the heart by their unexpected friendship, I stayed until a lunch bell called them away.

Dazed, I walked to the car, puzzling over what had happened. Suddenly, I remembered my prayer. I stopped, my hand on the door of the car, and I felt as if an earthquake was running through me from head to foot.

"Tell [God] all that is in your heart, as one unloads one's heart to a dear friend," wrote François Fénelon. "Tell him your troubles, that he may comfort you; tell him your joys, that he may sober them; tell him your longings, that he may purify them; tell him your mislikings, that he may help you conquer them; talk to him of your temptations, that he may shield you from them; show him all the wounds of your heart, that he may heal them. . . . Blessed are they who attain to such familiar, unreserved [communion] with God."[3]

When we open the minutes and hours of our days to him through our petitions, we open ourselves to the changes which can only be fashioned by his love. He can make a difference, right where we are, his touch, like sunlight, falling on our present surroundings.

5. Does Prayer Change Anything in the Lives of Those for Whom We Pray?

Martin Luther, when he felt particularly strong, was known to exclaim, "I feel as if I were being prayed for."[1]

Recently, a friend of ours, after making a difficult speech, called up to tell us, "Thank you— I felt your prayers."

There is no doubt that intercession is used by our Lord to reach, bless, and help those for whom we pray.

Albert Schweitzer once wrote that an individual can be "in his own world and in his own time, a simple channel of the power of Jesus."[2]

A young woman, doing volunteer work in a nursing home, encountered an aged man in a wheel chair whose heart and face were filled with bitterness.

It seems that his only surviving relatives lived far away, and, absorbed in their own families and pursuits, apparently had abandoned him to loneliness, rejection and despair. Worse, he had suffered financial reverses which he felt negated his professional career. Finally, there was the problem of his confinement to the wheel chair. A more hopeless situation one could hardly imagine. The young woman, however, having heard him out, asked if they might pray together.

"Why not?" the man shrugged dejectedly.

Knowing that she could neither talk away hurts so deep nor eradicate the circumstances that had caused them, she simply took his hand and asked God to remove from his heart the aching bitterness he had just revealed.

Following her prayer there was a healing of the old man's spirit. His face and attitude underwent a complete change. Within a week all trace of the bitterness vanished. A new sense of humor sparkled in him. His burden had been taken away.

His experience is one shared by many. Even if our circumstances can not be changed, yet we ourselves can be changed. The risen Christ can actually impart to us, often through the prayers of another, an inexpressible power of joy that transcends the hurts of this world.

Perhaps God's profoundest miracles are those that take place within the invisible depths of the human heart.

As we pray for others it is helpful to remember our true relationship with God. Our intellect, opinions, and accomplishments dwindle to insignificance before him who gave us all we have.

"We must come before him as paupers," a wise and white-haired seminary professor once advised. This is true in many respects, but especially is it true in the matter of intercession. There is so much we don't know.

Sometimes, when our intercession seems to go unanswered, it's possible, for instance, that the hour for its fulfillment has not yet come. We might need to discard our own time-plan and persist in prayer.

A friend told me how, after many years of indecision, he finally joined a church. When he informed his sister of his new commitment he was startled by her response. It seems that, for over twenty years, she had been praying for him to join a church.

There is a timing in the way of things that is of God. There is a knowledge of the person for whom we pray that is his alone. Whenever, aware of his greater understanding, we seek, in all humility, to align our will with his, the results can be so vivid as to make us feel the Book of Acts continues unbroken into this century.

Some years ago, I was introduced to a man who, as he shook my hand, stared over my shoulder in a cold and markedly bored fashion, as if looking about for someone more interesting.

Later, I was with a group of people who brought up the subject of this man, citing instances of his pride and criticizing him for his arrogance. I considered joining in with the story of my own encounter with him but, for some reason, I didn't. Instead, I turned my thoughts to God and silently asked, "Father?" The answer came, not in words audible to the ear, but quietly within my heart, that I should pray for him.

When I returned home, I wondered how to form my intercession. Finally it came to me, with certainty, that I should ask for Christ to touch his heart.

Without telling anyone about it, I continued this prayer for him for many years. In all that time he never spoke to me, nor did he have reason to, nor I to him.

One evening, at a large party, I paused on my way from the buffet table to scan the crowded room for Bill. Suddenly I was aware that the man for whom I had been praying so long had come up and was standing beside me.

I didn't know what to say, but I needn't have been concerned, for it was he who began to talk.

Balancing my plate of too many refreshments, I listened as he chatted amiably about the party, some of the people there, and what a fine man my husband was.

Then, as I stood poised in an unforgettable moment of wonder, he began to pour out to me how Christ had touched his heart.

"When . . . a soul throws in its dominant desire alongside God's," wrote Harry Emerson Fosdick, "no one easily can set boundaries to that prayer's influence."[3]

There are those, in fact, whose prayers have made a difference in many thousands of lives.

On a trip to Honduras, a San Antonio stockbroker was deeply moved by the devastation wrought there following a severe hurricane. As he tried to return to his profession, he was constantly troubled by the memory of the homeless, orphaned and suffering.

The words of our Lord pursued him: "I was naked and ye clothed me . . . hungry and ye fed me . . . inasmuch as you have done it unto the least of these my brethren ye have done it unto me."

Finally, he resolved to dedicate the following year mainly to relief efforts in Honduras. His first specific task came in the form of an urgent request for bandages in the Honduran leper colony. The needed bandages would cost one thousand dollars.

"Where to go from here?" he puzzled. "And how?"

It was one thing to participate, as he so often had, in college and church fund-raising drives and quite another to strike out on his own looking for money for lepers in a land remote from the experience of most of the people he knew. He felt, however, that the Lord who had drawn him into this work would guide him through it.

He went to a nearby church and knelt in silent prayer, asking for the grace to meet the lepers' need. He left with a feeling of peace.

Less than an hour later a friend unexpectedly called from a distant city. He and his wife had heard about the stockbroker's interest in the relief efforts in Honduras and wanted to know if they could be of help.

"Well, as a matter of fact," he began, "I'm looking for a thousand dollars for bandages. If any part of that—"

"It's yours," responded his friend. "We'd like to give it all. We've been wanting to do something."

The words of Elizabeth Barrett Browning could have been written for the stockbroker as he slowly put down the receiver.

> God answers sharp and sudden on some
>   prayers,
> And thrusts the thing we have prayed
>   for in our face,
> A gauntlet with a gift in it.[4]

The gift was not only an answer to his specific prayer but challenged him to continue the path he had started. It was the beginning of a chain of similar "coincidences"; hard work and travel through which literally thousands have received medical care, food, shelter and clothing.

It is a continuing wonder to me how the Father will take the clumsy, earthen conduits of our prayers and pour out his glory through them into the lives of others, not only in great things of far-reaching consequence but also in the smallest and most insignificant of instances.

Recently I had a series of miserable encounters with a grumpy saleslady in a shop near our home. The lady in question unfailingly went out of her way to be difficult and rude. One day I left the store and considered never returning. Yet this was a poor solution. So I began to consider what our Lord had to say about dealing with hostile people.

"Pray for those who despitefully use you," he had said.

"Did he mean to include," I considered, "grumpy salesladies?"

Dietrich Bonhoeffer once wrote, "The commandment of Jesus must be accorded perfect obedience in daily life and work."[5]

We reached the same conclusion, Bonhoeffer and I, but I suspect mine came through a much simpler mental process. I just decided that if I couldn't apply our Lord's words in the shopping center, I probably couldn't apply them anywhere.

"If you say so, I will," responded Peter when Jesus told him to let down his net again. With somewhat the same attitude I began to pray for the saleslady.

I prayed for her in the form of a blessing, asking that the love of our Lord come upon her and fill her and surround her and her loved ones. I prayed that only good come to her and thought of her immersed in the light and love of God.

The next time I went to the shop I hesitated at the door. I had a sinking sensation at the thought of another unpleasant encounter. Then, remembering my prayer, I opened the door.

As I entered, she came over to me, put out her arms, embraced me to her heart and said, "Hon!"

I was speechless. I had in no way changed. Her response could not have been to anything I was or did or had said. She could only have been drawn unthinkingly, instinctively, to the love of Christ as it came to her through my intercession.

"Prayer," wrote Tennyson, "is like opening a sluice between the great ocean and our little channels, when the sea gathers itself together and flows in at full tide."[6]

It is not only for people that we are called to be channels but for all of creation. St. Francis gave thanks and praise for sun, moon, earth, and stars. Teilhard de Chardin is said to have offered up the world in its entirety in prayer. Once I heard a dignified and saintly priest pray with feeling for the endangered blue whales.

Often, out of my own heart, intercession springs forth spontaneously for the cleansing and preservation of our air, water, and woodlands. Prayers for goodness and purity in the field of entertainment, for medical research, for our schools and colleges, for peace and world harmony—all have their place in intercession.

I interceded once on behalf of a small, insignificant garden. One weekend, several years ago, Bill dug me a little garden in front of our house. Knowing I lacked both experience and a green thumb, I began my planting with trepidation.

As I was tremulously inserting little bedding plants into the soil and adding what I hoped was neither too much nor too little water, a neighbor strolled up.

"So you're planting a garden," she observed dryly. "Well, it'll never work. If the bugs don't get it, the dogs will. Nobody can grow a garden around here."

As I looked up, amazed, she turned and started to walk off down the driveway. Then she stopped and called over her shoulder in parting, "By the way, before you moved here, your house was robbed three times."

I sat back on my heels and watched her go—rather glad to see her go, as a matter of fact. Then I looked down at my tiny periwinkles and pansies and up at our house, the home Bill and I had so carefully chosen to shelter our three children.

Bishop Cuthbert Bardsley of Coventry, England, once wrote of his own personal experience with "a living Lord who appeared to be interested in the little happenings of my uneventful life."[7]

It was to the living Lord I turned at that moment.

"Father," I prayed, "I give this garden to you. I ask your protection around it and over it. I ask that it prosper and bring joy to those who look upon it. And I ask that your angels circle and guard our home. In Jesus' name, Amen."

Despite my inexperience, the little garden flourished. To my surprise, strangers invited me to join their garden clubs. Friends and neighbors commented on the pleasure it gave them as they walked or drove by. On Christmas morning there was an unexpected gift in the overnight appearance of all the daffodils' first, lovely green shoots.

Bugs and dogs were never a problem, the house was not robbed, and perhaps, most remarkable of all, I never had a moment's fear that it would be.

Our intercessions can apply to all of life. I share Bonhoeffer's conviction that "Jesus claims for himself and the kingdom of God the whole of human life in all its manifestations."[8]

I love the advice of St. Isaac of Syria who recommended that we gather all of creation, even the birds and the animals, into the circle of our prayers.

Years ago, I was sitting on our kitchen floor, my arms around a great, wolflike German shepherd dog. Bill had given him to me over a year before. At the time he was an adorable bundle of fluff. But, in the ensuing months, Fafner, whom we named after a giant who guarded a treasure, matured into a likely resemblance of his namesake. So big he became, so aggressive and unmanageable, that we reluctantly realized our little house could no longer contain him.

We made several, unsuccessful attempts to find him a home more suited to his bold and restless personality. No one wanted him. Finally the Air Force agreed to try him as a sentry dog.

And so, on that day so many years ago, I was saying goodby to Fafner. A military crate labeled "CAUTION—U.S. SENTRY DOG" was beside me. An impersonal letter on my desk informed us that, if he proved satisfactory, we would receive a check and thereby release ownership.

As I stroked his rough, warm, furry coat my

eyes filled with tears. Instinctively I prayed for him. Despite the impossibility of keeping Fafner, I loved him. "Surely it's all right to pray for a dog," I thought. Had not God told us through the Psalms that "every beast of the forest is mine" (Ps. 50:10) and that "his tender mercies are over all his works"? (Ps. 145:9).

My prayer for him was not only that good would come to him but that, most especially, this beautiful animal, who looked so much like a "beast of the forest," would bring good to someone.

Shortly after we shipped him we received a check from the Air Force. We never expected to hear of Fafner again.

Six years later, during the war in Viet Nam, Bill brought in the mail with a puzzled look.

"This just came from Binh Thuy Air Base in Viet Nam," he said, leaning against the door and ripping open the envelope. "We don't know anyone over there, do we?"

We didn't—up until that moment. In a matter of a few seconds' reading, we became acquainted with a young soldier whose duty it was to patrol the perimeter of an air base during the hours of darkness with the help of an assigned sentry dog.

He must have gone to some trouble to locate our name and address in order to share with us a feeling of gratitude which just tumbled out over the pages. It seems that one night, during his lonely patrol, a dog named Fafner had saved his life.

When, years later, I came across these lines by Ethel Romig Fuller, I thought again of the prayer, the young man, and the dog:

If radio's slim fingers can pluck a melody
from night and toss it over continent or sea . . .
Why should mortals wonder if God hears prayer?"*

Sometimes our prayers for others take a surprising turn. Either our intercession so quickens our sensitivity to the person or situation that we find we must change our prayer or we feel motivated to take an action which otherwise would not have occurred to us.

One Thursday morning before Easter, as I was praying for Bill's eighty-year-old mother, there came an inner conviction that I should leave my prayers and call her on the phone.

Of all the people in the world, Bill's mother was one of those whom I loved most. Yet, since she lived far away, we seldom called each other. Instead we wrote frequently.

She was independent, living alone by choice. With the exception of a long-standing heart condition, she was remarkably well. She drove, did her own marketing and cooking, visited her

* Ethel Rommig Fuller, "Proof," from *Kitchen Sonnets* (Portland, Or.: Metropolitan Press, 1931).

friends and went to church. I knew of no reason to call her. Yet the conviction persisted.

When I phoned, I found her in an exceptionally happy frame of mind. She was delighted by the call and enjoyed the latest news about the children. We had what she would describe as "a real good talk." It was the kind we loved to have when we were together.

I put down the phone in a glow, so glad I had called, so grateful for those warm minutes together.

That afternoon she suddenly and unexpectedly passed away. There is no way in the world that I could have known this would happen. Yet our Lord surely knew and, knowing, took my morning prayer and transformed it into an action for which I will ever be grateful.

One aspect of prayer for others is the effect it has on the intercessor. "Intercession sincerely and habitually practiced will have notable results in the one who prays," wrote Harry Emerson Fosdick.[9] There is a tendency to become more caring, more aware, more forgiving. It is as if by touching our Lord with our requests for others we also are touched by his love for them.

Yet, there may be some who, having read thus far, still feel as the psalmist once did: "I cry . . . but thou hearest not" (Ps. 22:2).

Perhaps they question their ever having been a channel of God's love to another. Maybe they are not aware of ever experiencing an answer to any kind of prayer at all.

It is especially to them that the next chapter is dedicated.

6. The Secret of Answered Prayer

"My prayer wasn't answered," a young man told me. "I prayed and prayed for that person," someone else said, "but nothing happened." A woman once commented wistfully, "Saints' prayers are answered—not mine."

Why is it that some people experience fulfillment in prayer, closeness to God, and evident answers while others do not? Is it because the former are "saints" in the popular sense of the word and somehow different from the rest of us? Or is there a key to prayer, a clue?

A young housewife was faced with a divorce

she had neither sought nor wanted. Grief-stricken, she prayed earnestly, even desperately, that her marriage be saved. Yet, in spite of her prayers and all she said or did, the divorce became final.

She was left with little money, small children to care for, and a pressing need to seek employment. Filled with a deep anxiety concerning her future and pursued by feelings of failure and rejection, she came close to despair.

She had reached a point where many stumble and fall. Regarding prayer only as a means whereby they might obtain their desires, they become angry, frustrated, sometimes abandoning prayer altogether. The young woman, however, came to a deeper, more accurate understanding of the meaning of prayer.

A successful quarterback in professional football once credited the precision of his passes to the discipline of his vision. By an act of will and courage he "blurs out" the rush of defensive linemen and focuses on his receivers. By a similar act of will and courage the young housewife chose a new point of focus.

She "blurred out" her initial, despairing vision of her situation. Instead, she "saw" the love, light, and caring of God as being very present to her in the reality of her brokenness.

With prayer and faith, seeking his guidance and strength in all things, she dared to claim his incredible promise that she was not alone. In this light, she could even accept the possibility that, in spite of all that had happened, there still might be beautiful blessings in store for her and her children.

As she continued to dip her little cup deeply into the very Fountain of Life, a measure of peace and hope began to fill her. She found a job suited to her gifts and training and a less expensive house adequate to the needs of her children. Beyond the house, just visible from her kitchen window, rose a line of distant hills. As she prepared meals, she often whispered softly the words of the psalmist, "I will lift up mine eyes unto the hills, from whence cometh my help. My help cometh from the Lord, which made heaven and earth" (Ps. 121:1–2).

And the help did come. There flowed through her such strength as not only held herself and her little family together but poured out into her relationships with others, giving her success in her job and drawing to her many wonderful friends.

Looking back, she could see that, although the specific prayer for her marriage had not been granted, for reasons she might never be able to understand in this life, yet her underlying prayer for help in a situation which threatened to overwhelm her had been more than granted.

There is, in truth, a secret to prayer—a secret not in the sense that it has been hidden from us, but in the sense that we have hidden ourselves from it.

Years ago, when our preschoolers had to spend long winter days indoors, they often released energy in games of hide-and-seek. I was intrigued, and sometimes annoyed, by their creativity in discovering new ways to hide from one another.

One particularly rainy afternoon I opened my closet to get my coat only to discover it, and most of the rest of my clothes, tumbled on the floor in a great, bouncing, mobile heap of dresses, skirts, and blouses totally concealing someone small who whispered, "Sh-h-h."

Like children, we too are ingenious at concealment. We pray from beneath a veritable mountain of desires, hopes, plans, projects, anxieties, and demands. The secret of answered prayer waits, like a silent star, for us to put aside the coverings and notice it.

"Our Father who art in heaven," Jesus taught us to pray, "Hallowed be thy name. Thy kingdom come. Thy will be done . . ." (Matt. 6:9–13).

One of the greatest treasures tucked within these lines is the new focus it gives us, a center point not in ourselves and our frustrations but in the Father and his will. His opening sentences provide not only precise words with which to start prayer but also a pattern to follow. First, we are to revere God's name; second, to seek his way.

Such a beginning necessarily colors the rest of our prayer, putting our needs, regrets, and concerns into perspective. Within those first phrases which our Lord has given us can be found the secret of answered prayer.

But how, in an ordinary, everyday sense, might we apply it?

Recently, I discovered that a young woman who had been coming to help me with the ironing had some problems. I resolved to assist her in any way I could. Many opportunities came, but one of them I can only describe as "the little miracle of the slacks."

I was going through my closet one morning when my only pair of warm woolen slacks caught my attention.

"Lord," I silently objected, "not my slacks! Surely you don't want me to give her those? You know they're the only pair I've got."

My prayer, though an unlikely candidate for an illuminated manuscript, was in reality one of adoration and followed the guidelines laid out in the opening phrases of the Lord's prayer. For, in essence, underneath the surface words, I was saying, "Father, I hold your name in reverence, and your will, in spite of all my reluctance, demurring, and muttering, matters to me more than my own."

As I hesitated by the clothes rack, I became

aware that, while I only occasionally wear slacks, my helper wore them all the time to do her work. Further, though I was glad to have them when I happened to feel like wearing them, she actually needed them.

Sören Kierkegaard once flung the New Testament challenge into the words, "What thou shalt do is to follow Christ."[1]

Well, as I took my only pair of warm slacks off the hanger and gave them away, I was, in that small moment of time, trying.

A remarkable addendum to this story came a few days later. A good friend called. "I have this darling pair of slacks with matching jacket," she said. "I've—let's put it this way—outgrown them. I was wondering what in the world to do, and it occurred to me, since you wear a smaller size, you might possibly be able to use them."

I tried them on. They were just as warm, fit me better, and looked prettier than the ones I had given away. It was the only time, in my entire life, I have ever received a gift of slacks.

Prayer, in accord with Jesus' guidelines, puts us into communion. It is no longer a question of our request versus his refusal, but rather of our reverence and obedience coming into oneness with his outreaching love.

"In this response of self-giving," wrote the

theologian Emil Brunner, " . . . actual fellowship between God and man originates."[2]

Several years ago some friends of ours were on a vacation in New York City. The purpose of their trip was purely fun. It was to be a restful and restoring time away from the responsibilities of home. They had looked forward to it with delight.

But it didn't turn out the way they had planned. The first morning there they had an argument. They parted for the day's previously planned activities in anger—she to shop, he to attend to some business.

During the morning the young wife was too miserable to enjoy her shopping. After lunch, walking back to her hotel, she passed a church. Her thoughts ceased spinning around her unhappiness and refocused on our Lord.

She had loved Jesus since she was a child. It was not so much that she now wanted to get something from him. She simply desired to be with him and to offer to him what it was she had with her at that time—her distress.

Spontaneously, she entered the church. It turned out to be a beautiful old building, dimly lit; a service of Holy Communion was in progress. Kneeling, she lifted up her heart.

"Come unto me," Jesus had said, ". . . and I will refresh you" (Matt. 11:28).

She believed him. In his light she began to see her situation differently. Her hurt receded. Her loneliness was touched by his nearness. Her inner turmoil quieted into peace; her anger melted into understanding, and a great calm fell across her memory of the morning's argument.

Comforted, she resumed her seat as the service proceeded. Out of a city of eight million people there was no way to hope her husband might be there also, yet she longed to share with him what she was feeling.

When it was time for the participants to go forward to receive the bread and wine a small miracle took place. It went unnoticed by the congregation. In fact, only two people were aware of it. The young woman and her husband met, quite by chance, at the altar rail.

It is by such open-hearted turning to God as theirs, in even our smallest concerns, that we begin to experience fulfillment in prayer.

I am reminded of the words from a familiar Christmas hymn:

Where meek souls will receive Him, still
the dear Christ enters in.[3]

He is a living Lord who thus "enters" and One whose arrival makes a remarkable difference.

I remember some time ago being at my wit's end trying to know how to deal with an apparently unreasonable individual. I hoped the person would change, but my prayers in this direction went unanswered.

Perplexed, I put aside my own idea of the solution—that this particular individual "sharpen up"—and prayed instead for guidance. Shortly thereafter several books happened to come into my hands. They all dealt with loving and accepting others just as they are, and the giving of thanks for them as part of that acceptance.

One day, after a particularly strained encounter, I decided to apply what I had been reading. I felt that through these books I was discovering the Father's will for me in this specific relationship.

I went to a place where I could be alone, knelt down, and by an act of will put aside my critical attitude and gave thanks for the individual.

As I did, I was granted the light to see with a sparkling clarity that this person possessed admirable qualities to which I had been blind. I completely changed my attitude in the relationship and experienced an immediate and corresponding warmth in return.

Our Lord desires not only to enter each one of our lives and to conform us to his will, but also to reach out to others through us.

There is a city hospital which has the reputation of giving medical students experience with almost every illness known to man.

Everything from flu to leprosy passes between its dingy walls. Even prisoners, their ankle chains dragging, shuffle along the corridors to be treated. It is a semi-charity hospital—inadequate, understaffed, available for people who can't afford a family doctor. Recently, I worked there as a volunteer.

One day, as I was running errands around the hospital for the nurses, I quietly lifted up my heart to God the Father. "Where," I silently asked him, looking at all the shabbiness and suffering, "is your love in this place?" There was an answer. It came instantly.

To my right was a treatment room; I noticed at that moment two people: an orderly in a uniform intended to be crisp but, at this point in the day, crumpled; and a young doctor. The latter was perspiring, tight-lipped, and pale with his effort to do a neat, conscientious job of stitching the injury of a child. Simultaneously the orderly, though a large and rugged man, was ever so tenderly toweling off the little girl's face.

I will not soon forget his expression of compassion, nor the way he began gently, unself-consciously, to sing to the child as a father might croon to his baby.

In that brief moment of time and space, in one small forgotten corner of this earth, an event of healing and kindness was taking place. I realized, as I stood watching, just how completely each of us, whatever our sphere of influence, can become incarnate expressions of God's love.

"The issue is not whether the Lord can make a difference," wrote Lloyd John Ogilvie, "but whether we will allow him to make his difference through us."[4]

Becoming clear channels of his will, both in prayer and action, requires our periodically "returning to the Source."

Several years ago I was embroiled in a whirl of commitments. "Come ye . . . apart into a desert place, and rest a while," Jesus once advised his disciples (Mark 6:31). A dear friend of ours advised the same thing in the form of sending me the unexpected gift of a plane ticket to a weekend retreat in New Mexico.

Surprised, amazed, protesting to my family about the impossibility of taking the time to go or of accepting so generous a present, I found myself, nevertheless, on my way to the retreat.

There, with a charming room to myself, a fascinating desert to stroll in, and beautiful meditations presented throughout the day by a gifted Episcopal priest, I received a new outlook.

"It is not," said our leader, "your business here with our Lord that matters at all, but his business with you."

As the weekend progressed, I became increasingly aware of how overcommitted I had become. It occurred to me that it was possible to drop some things, to slow down, to spend more time with the children who all too soon would be grown up. I saw the advantage—in fact, for me the imperative—of trying to do a few things well rather than many things in haste. I returned home with the courage to make the needed changes, full of joy and a heart more centered in Christ.

Even without a retreat experience, just temporarily putting aside our specific and identifiable prayer requests in order to refresh ourselves in Scripture, literature, and with those who love the Lord can affect us as a tall antenna does our television. We go from confused to clear.

A few months ago I rushed into the house carrying several sacks of groceries. Going around in my head was the menu for that night. It was late afternoon and I was in a hurry to get dinner started. As I came in the phone was ringing. Putting down the groceries, I lifted the receiver. A friend was on the other end, calling to remind us of a family supper to be held at our church that night.

After we hung up, I went back to put the groceries away. Everything had changed. I approached them in a different manner. I was no longer rushed. The menu faded into unimportance. We wouldn't be having dinner at home after all. Because I had stopped long enough to listen on the phone, my focus had changed.

Just the simple fact of taking time to be alone with our Lord will have its inevitable effect.

Several years ago Bill and I realized how difficult it had become to carry on a sustained in-depth conversation with each other amidst the almost symphonic complexity of sound in our household.

The comings and goings of three teenaged children, punctuated by slamming doors, thumping feet, laughter, and the voices of their friends, made up but a part. The strains of stereo, telephone, and piano intermingled far into the night with such things as the staccato bark of their beagle and an occasional shriek, siren, or earthquake from the television. The sum total made up one, long—albeit joyful—interruption.

In self-defense, we decided that just the two of us would go out for breakfast every Saturday morning to share a peaceful interlude.

The idea was so successful that we have continued the practice for many years. How differently we have related to each other, our children, and those around us because of the decisions and understandings we reached during these quiet times together each Saturday morning.

"Who rises from prayer a better man," wrote George Meredith, "his prayer is answered."[5] As prayer is ever communion with One greater than ourselves, we can count on this aspect of prayer fulfillment.

One summer, in support of a program being conducted by our church, I volunteered to teach a class of underprivileged children. In my particular class I discovered a wide range of students from clean, bright, and cooperative to unwashed, unloved, backward, rebellious, superstitious, and despairing.

The first day my inexperience crashed into the stone wall of this challenge and got nowhere. After class, depressed, scared, and wishing I'd never signed up for the program, I went into the church to spend some time by myself with our Lord.

In deep reverence, love, and trust I offered him both myself and the class. As I sat alone, I gradually became aware of a series of stained glass windows illustrating the Twenty-third Psalm, high above the altar. I had never really looked at them before. I got up and walked slowly from one to another, absorbing the message depicted in the glass made luminous by the afternoon sun.

As I reached the last, I realized anew that I was not alone, that I had a Shepherd. The realization went deep into me, into the emotional part where one's anxieties whirl, and there followed a wonderful calm. It was as if the Lord had stretched forth his hand and once more quieted a stormy sea. I left the church feeling assured that he would be with me as I taught the children.

Adoration of our Lord motivating, underlying, infusing our prayers, changing them from self-centered to God-centered, draws us into the current of his will and carries us into answers beyond our imaginings. Further, he receives our self-offerings, no matter how tentative, small, and weak with tenderness.

I recently heard the story of a young minister and his wife who were expecting their bishop's first visit to their home. The day he was to arrive was devoted to cleaning, polishing, and scrubbing. Many hours were spent in the kitchen as preparations for a dinner party in his honor were brought to completion.

Finally, late in the afternoon, the house ready, the dinner cooked, the table resplendent with the best china, glass, and silver, the young wife retired to the kitchen to put the finishing touches on a bouquet of flowers she was arranging as a centerpiece.

The family's little daughter, having observed the table without a centerpiece, had vanished into the backyard to make some preparations of her own.

The father waited in the living room, peering through the blinds from time to time lest the bishop be kept waiting even a moment at the door.

He arrived a little earlier than the minister's wife expected. Just as she was walking into the dining room carrying the bouquet of flowers for the table, the bishop and her husband entered the living room. Simultaneously their small daughter came in by another door. The four of them paused, looking at one another, for an instant. The little girl was holding a saucer on which a number of dandelions had been painstakingly arranged.

In that moment a kind of loving communion flowed among them. Without a word the mother quietly withdrew into the kitchen with her centerpiece.

That night a delicious dinner was served, the guests were delighted, and the best china, glass, and silver sparkled in their hands.

On the center of the table was a saucer of dandelions.

"Our Father, . . . hallowed be thy name. Thy kingdom come. Thy will be done. . . ." A simple beginning, as simple as a child's offering of wildflowers, yet containing the whole heart and secret of prayer.

7. Pegs to Hang Our Prayers On

Take time to be holy
Speak oft with thy Lord . . .[1]

Old-fashioned lines—how do they apply to you and me? The word *holy* in its Old English derivation implies wholeness. Time we spend in prayer inevitably leads to a greater degree of personal wholeness. Richard Trench expressed something of this in his words:

Lord, what a change within us one short hour
Spent in Thy presence will avail to make . . .[2]

Yet, if we take time to be alone with our Lord, the cogent question arises, "How do we pray?" And, for many—more pertinent still—where in our busy, distracting, whirling lives do we find an hour of solitude?

Our great need for daily devotions is readily apparent. We feel it in our spirits. There is a hunger akin to bodily hunger, a desire for the feeding of the "inner man." Jesus knew of this hunger; his lifestyle included a regular pattern of withdrawal for prayer and reentry for service.

> They who have steeped their souls in
>   prayer
> Can every anguish calmly bear.[3]

Most of us know people such as the ones described in this poem by Richard Milnes, men and women of prayer who consistently reveal a strength not of themselves. Their actions, reactions, and very countenances reflect a close relationship with the living Lord.

I'll never forget an engineer who regarded the Christian faith with skepticism. One day he happened to meet the minister of his wife's church. Shortly thereafter he became a dedicated Christian.

"What happened?" I asked him.

"I wanted to have," he said, "what I saw in that man's face."

"We kneel, how weak!" wrote Richard Trench. "We rise, how full of power!"[4]

Even so, the pragmatic realities of finding the time can present a problem.

"I don't know what to plant in my garden," I once confided in a friend.

"Drive around the neighborhood and see what other people are planting," came her logical response.

In the same spirit, let me share with you the manner in which three of the busiest people I know have found time for daily prayer.

A businessman, who was working an eleven-hour day and was, in addition, deeply involved in church, community, and college-related positions of leadership, found time for prayer each morning before he awakened his wife and children.

He set his alarm thirty minutes early and, in the silence of dawn, read from his Bible and prayed. He found he was not burdened by this practice but rather strengthened, renewed, and given a more clear perspective.

A housewife, with active school-age children, many civic and church commitments, and a busy, involved husband, sought time for prayer. She found it in the brief calm following her husband's and children's departure in the morning.

Before the phone started ringing, before the housework, before even dressing for the day, she would spend a quiet few minutes in prayer and devotional reading.

It is interesting to note that she is an individual to whom many are drawn because of the comfort, warmth, and love which seem to flow from her at all times.

A working mother of teenagers, with a dynamic husband whose profession included some entertaining at home, was challenged more than most to find time for prayer. Physically exhausted by the demands on her, but still mentally stimulated in the evening, she propped herself up in bed each night to be fed by the words of her Bible and to be strengthened through a few minutes of prayer.

She is one through whom the love of God has touched countless lives in a particularly tender and beautiful way.

But finding the time is only one step in the experience of daily devotions. How we use it is yet another, and to many, the hardest part.

Suppose that you have decided to spend half an hour in prayer. Let us say you are in a relatively quiet place. Perhaps you can hear a clock ticking somewhere, a car passing, a lawn mower in the distance, but otherwise you are in stillness. You expect no interruptions. At this point you may wonder how to proceed.

How do we approach our Lord, in what patterns form our prayers, with what words address him? There are some helpful pegs on which to hang our prayers, some simple arrangements of thoughts and feelings that can be of assistance.

First of all, before we begin to pray, in order to distract our minds from our preoccupations, it can be helpful to quietly read from the Bible or a devotional book. This can bring about a refocusing of our thoughts, a recentering on our Lord, a concentration of our personality Godward.

Some people are hesitant to try the Bible, but it isn't really a difficult book to read. As a matter of fact, a child can read it. Picking up the Psalms, you will find yourself, your own feelings expressed in them. Reading through the Gospels, you may find puzzling passages, stories or expressions you lack the historical background to comprehend, but, in the main, you will receive what our Lord intends to give you—an awareness that he loves you and that his will for you is to love others. The Bible has been well described as a "love letter to us from God."

In addition to reading devotional material, you may find it helpful to list and quietly read over the attributes of God as he has been revealed to us through Jesus, such as "light," "truth," "mercy," "compassion" and so on.

Following reading—or without it—we can choose from methods of prayer as infinite in number as the stars and varied enough to cover every mood and need and condition of our spirits. I would like to share with you a very few, found to be real and helpful to the kind of people who live down the street from you, walk through your supermarket, and pass you at the traffic light.

Perhaps the first and most natural peg on which to hang any prayer consists of our own words as they express our relationship to God at the time of speaking. Alone in our quiet time, we might "tell it like it is."

> Lord, I'm here. I want to know you. Please show me how. Lord, I'm worried about my loved one. Please help him. And, Lord, I'm really sorry about the way I talked to him this morning. And, Lord, please, Lord, help me to just be a better person. Amen.

This unstudied approach to God applies not only to ordinary situations but also to times of crisis. A friend of ours told us of her own experience with this kind of prayer.

"God, I don't understand anything about you at all," she prayed several years ago, "but I give you now all that I am." At that time she lay paralyzed, unable to speak, suffering the excruciating agony of withdrawal from a fourteen-year dependence on drugs and alcohol.

She felt, at the moment of her prayer, for the first time in her life, the presence of God. She was sustained by him, "in every molecule of my being," she later told us. She recovered, totally healed of an addiction that had earlier been pronounced incurable by her physician. Today she speaks gratefully of the Lord's reality and closeness.

The essence of her prayer was honesty, a peg on which any of us, at any time in our lives, can hang a prayer. Simplicity is another.

A soldier in World War II was concealed in a hut during a raging nighttime blizzard. Suddenly the roof collapsed, exposing him both to the enemy and the ruthless cold.

"At that moment," the soldier recently told me, "I saw more clearly than I can describe how completely I had turned my back on the Lord, and I cried out, 'God, I'm yours!' "

His instant commitment on the battlefield led to a relationship with Christ which has not only lasted some thirty years but shines from his face, is reflected in his actions, and is the center of his successful and happy marriage.

A simple prayer, sincerely spoken, is heard, received, and honored by our Father in heaven more than all the exalted, long and flowery expressions of a soul less honest.

"Words without thoughts never to heaven go," wrote Shakespeare.[5] It is not our phrases but our hearts God looks upon.

"What does the average churchman most want in a minister?" a prominent layman was asked at a clergy conference.

"A man who is for real," came the immediate answer.

So does our Lord look for a man or woman in prayer who is "for real."

Bishop Taylor Smith of England gave us a masterpiece of simplicity in his prayer:

> Dear Lord,
> This day—
> for Thee,
> for them,
> Amen.

Truly desired, his words can form for us a powerful, life-changing petition.

"Lord, have mercy upon me, a sinner" . . . "Father, help me through this day" . . . "Lord, use me." Whether expressed in our own words or another's, such simple prayers, honestly meant, will always be answered.

Several years ago a friend shared with me an approach to prayer which offers a particularly helpful peg. The method is called ACTS.[6]

Adoration
Confession
Thanksgiving
Supplication

Guided in the order shown above, we proceed in our own way through each classification.

The words of Thomas Moore express so well something of the beauty of the first step, adoration.

> As down in the sunless retreats of the
>   ocean
> Sweet flowers are springing no mortal
>   can see
> So, deep in my soul the still prayer of
>   devotion
> Unheard by the world, rises silent to
>   Thee.[7]

Those "flowers . . . no mortal can see" will have their effect. True love for God shows, and, in the words of Catherine Doherty, "the presence of a person who is in love with God is enough. . . ."[8] Spending time in adoration will not only make a difference in us, but through us, as we return to our daily pursuits.

Confession deals with the reality of our constant stumbling. It is grand to confess, to be lifted up by God, dusted off, and set on our way again with a fresh start.

Thanksgiving follows confession. I cannot say

why it is that "an attitude of gratitude" toward our Creator opens us both to perceive and receive his gifts and blessings while the opposite attitude has the reverse effect, but it is so nevertheless. Cultivating wonder and a thankful, trusting heart "in all things" opens us to joy, while harboring a negative, ungrateful spirit will attract misery like a magnet.

Last of all comes supplication, our prayers for ourselves and others.

One spring I attended a small study group in our church. Between our weekly meetings we decided to pray for one another every day. A member of the group was a widow who lived alone.

"Each night," she said, "as I went to bed, I thought to myself, 'Twelve people are praying for me this day.' I cannot tell you what it meant to me."

Our intercessions, whether the one for whom we pray is aware of them or not, are a part of the ministry of the love of Christ through us.

As we come to our own needs, it doesn't hurt to remember the advice of John Tyler Pettee:

> Pray for peace and grace and spiritual
>   food,
> For wisdom and guidance, for all these
>   are good,
> But don't forget the potatoes.[9]

Our supplications can be very real, very honest, right out of where we are.

Recently a young waitress at a restaurant where we were having dinner told us of her prayer for employment. "I want to go to college full-time," she said, "but first I have to earn the money. I prayed about it and the doors started opening and here I am with just the perfect job."

Countless Christians can testify to needs having been met through honest supplication.

On a retreat I discovered a peg that involved making the Lord's prayer specific for someone else:

"Our Father who art in heaven, hallowed be thy name [in (name of person)]. Thy kingdom come, thy will be done, on earth as it is in heaven [in (name)]. Give [him/her] this day [his/her] daily bread . . ." and so on throughout the prayer.

Other pegs can be found in the form of books or pamphlets of prayer. "Pray in the darkness if there be no light," wrote Hartley Coleridge.[10] A bishop of our church told a group of us one evening how, with the help of such a peg, he had done just that.

"There have been times in my ministry when I was exhausted, empty, and spiritually dry," he said. "Then I just hung onto this book and it helped me through." In his hands was a book of prayers for morning, noon, and night and almost every occasion, a book which had made available to him the strength of many generations of believers.

Collections of prayers are available in abundance and can be a great support and guide when our own wells are dry.

Hymns, surprisingly, can serve as pegs. Many of the greatest hymns were originally prayers set to verse. Slowly and thoughtfully reading such ones as "Breathe on me, breath of God" or "Dear Lord and Father of Mankind"[11] can both reveal to ourselves and express to God the yearnings of our hearts.

Another helpful peg is the use of the Bible as our prayer book. Conforming our will to our Lord's, we might pray, for instance, something like this out of the fifteenth chapter of the Gospel of John:

> Lord, you are the vine. I pray to be a branch. I ask to abide in you and you in me that, by your grace, I may bring forth much fruit, for without you I can do nothing.

Or, perhaps, in time of stress we might turn to one of God's promises. For example, one morning, prior to the funeral of a close friend, I felt, for the first time, the meaning of the expression "weight of grief." So heavy was the burden on my spirit that I felt incapable of picking up the day's challenge.

Remembering the Beatitudes, I opened my Bible to the Sermon on the Mount and prayed in the words of our Lord, "Blessed are they that mourn: for they shall be comforted" (Matt. 5:4), adding, simply, "Lord, I mourn, may your Holy Spirit, the Comforter, grant me this promised comfort. In Jesus' name, Amen."

Later, at the memorial service, the burden of grief was completely taken away and replaced with an overwhelming gratitude for the life of our friend and a quiet sense that, somehow, all was well with him. The feeling has remained to this moment. The unbearable weight of sorrow never returned.

There are those who carry prayer out of their quiet time into all of their hours and are, as a dedicated surgeon put it to me recently concerning himself, "more or less in continuous prayer."

We have a charming friend who runs a flower shop. "Her eyes," in the words of Tennyson, "are homes of silent prayer."[12] Throughout the day, as she recognizes the hand of the Father at work, she quietly whispers, along with her beautiful smile, "Thank you, God."

A young Catholic priest we know prays constantly, as he walks down the street, for the people who pass him. "Bless you," he prays. "Father, bless this one . . . and that one, Lord, who just went by." "These faces," he said one time, "have you looked at them? So many of them need him."

Another friend, who has a vital ministry in the Episcopal Church, silently and prayerfully affirms as he talks with people, "God loves you and I love you." I have never known a man through whom the redeeming power of God flows more fully.

A movement toward more continuous prayer can begin with a series of set, planned times of prayer throughout the day.

On awakening, our first thought can be something like, "Blessed be the name of the Lord." Then, even before getting out of bed, we might offer ourselves, our day, and our loved ones to him.

Later, we could set apart an hour or twenty minutes' time for prayer and devotional reading.

In addition, some people use little reminders to turn their hearts to him as they go about their work—hearing the noon whistle, passing a particular church, or glimpsing a Christian symbol they wear. I have a cross by my washing machine which serves the same purpose.

In the evening, before bed, we might review our day before him, asking forgiveness, giving thanks, committing ourselves and our loved ones once more into his hands. This nightly process has often sent me back to someone in my family to ask their pardon or express my love for them.

Continuous prayer is a peg to reach for, one which can be touched by following the suggestion of Jane Cross Simpson when she joyfully wrote:

Go, when the morning shineth;
Go, when the noon is bright;
Go, when the eve declineth;
Go, in the high of night;
Go with pure mind and feeling,
Fling earthly cares away,
And in thy chamber kneeling,
Do thou in secret pray.[13]

Within the confines of this chapter are but a few of a great variety of pegs available for the arrangement of our prayers. In the following pages you will find prayers of beauty, insight, and wisdom, many of which were lovingly written by individuals whose relationship with God was extraordinarily transparent. May they be a light to you, as they have been to me.

But may you, at the same time, remember that prayer, whatever verbal form it takes, is a gift from God, and that not just to a few. It is for all his children, as much for the deaf, the illiterate, and the lost as for the eloquent, the wise, and the righteous. It is a means by which those who have stumbled may arise, those who are proud may be humbled, those who are weak may become strong. It is a way of relationship, the opening of a window between ourselves and the light of God.

8. Lighthouse Prayers

"I have the prayer," wrote a friend, "on my refrigerator, where amid menus, recipes, and grocery lists it meets me where my anxieties surface most evidently."

Her response was to a prayer I had given her— one written in the 1600s by a French bishop noted for his clarity of thought and devotion to God. Little did the author suppose, when he expressed his trust in our Lord so long ago, that one day his words would strengthen a twentieth-century housewife from the vantage point of her refrigerator door.

There are prayers written across the ages by individuals whose love for God is extraordinarily luminous; prayers that can shine for us like a lighthouse and guide us as effectively. Making them our own and persisting in them, we can find assistance in just about any situation that might confront us.

Not only can such prayers give verbal expression to our needs and desires and provide a crystalline focus to some of our hitherto vague yearnings but they can also give us the strengthening relationship of the many who have regarded their world and their Lord across the ages with hearts akin to our own.

The selections that follow speak for themselves. Moving from the natural concerns, feelings, anxieties, and overcomings common to us all, they progress into prayers of profound dedication and self-offering.

Perhaps you will decide to use some of them. If so, may you come by means of them, as have countless others before us, into an ever-increasing experience of the love and Presence of God in your life.

Help, Lord . . .

—Psalm 12:1

Have mercy upon me, O Lord; for I am weak . . .

Psalm 6:2

Lord our God . . . cleanse our bodies and souls, our hearts and consciences, that with a pure heart, and a clear soul, with perfect love and calm hope, we may venture confidently and fearlessly to pray unto Thee.

Coptic Liturgy of St. Basil, A.D. 370

Create in me a clean heart, O God; and renew a right spirit within me.

Psalm 51:10

O Lord, who hast mercy upon all, take away from me my sins, and mercifully kindle in me the fire of thy Holy Spirit. Take away from me the heart of stone, and give me a heart of flesh, a heart to love and adore Thee, a heart to delight in Thee, to follow and enjoy Thee, for Christ's sake.

St. Ambrose, 4th century

O Lord, my God, Light of the blind, and Strength of the weak; yea also, Light of those that see, and Strength of the strong; hearken unto my soul, and hear it crying out of the depths. . . . Light my candle, enlighten my darkness . . . for Thou art the true light that lighteth every man that cometh into the world.

St. Augustine, 5th century

Great Master, touch us with Thy skillful hand;
   Let not the music that is in us die!
Great Sculptor, hew and polish us; nor let,
   Hidden and lost, Thy form within us lie!

Horatius Bonar, "The Master's Touch," 19th century

Set a watch, O Lord, before my mouth; Keep the door of my lips . . . incline not my heart to any evil thing. . . .

Psalm 141:3–4

O holy Child of Bethlehem!
   Descend to us, we pray;
Cast out our sin and enter in,
   Be born in us today.

Phillips Brooks, "O Little Town of Bethlehem," 1867

. . . We, who are born in Christ,
A people pure from stain,
Praise we our God again,
   Lord of our peace!

Clement of Alexandria, 1st century

Thy nature, gracious Lord, impart;
   Come quickly from above;
Write thy new name upon my heart,
   Thy new, best name of Love.

Charles Wesley, "O For a Heart to Praise My God," 1742

O Lord our God . . . show us the course wherein
we should go . . . and guide and enable us unto
that which is our true good, to keep thy laws,
and in all our works evermore to rejoice in thy
glories and gladdening Presence. For thine is the
glory and praise . . . for ever and ever.

St. Basil, A.D. 370

Lead, kindly Light, . . .
   Lead Thou me on;
The night is dark, and I am far from home,
   Lead Thou me on.
Keep Thou my feet; I do not ask to see
The distant scene, one step enough for me.

Cardinal John Newman, "The Pillar of Cloud," 1833

O Lord my God, in thee do I put my trust.

Psalm 7:1

. . . Joy and strength and courage are with Thee. . . .

Archbishop Richard Trench, "Prayer," 19th century

Whither shall I go from thy spirit? or whither shall I flee from thy presence?

If I ascend up into heaven, thou art there; if I make my bed in hell, behold, thou art there.

If I take the wings of the morning, and dwell in the uttermost parts of the sea;

Even there shall thy hand lead me, and thy right hand shall hold me.

Psalm 139:7–10

Dear Lord, of thee three things I pray:
To see thee more clearly,
Love thee more dearly,
Follow thee more nearly. . . .

St. Richard of Chichester, "Day by Day," 13th century

God be in my head,
And in my understanding;

God be in my eyes,
  And in my looking;
God be in my mouth,
  And in my speaking;
God be in my heart,
  And in my thinking;
God be at my end,
  And at my departing.

Old Sarum Primer, 1558

Jesus at my right hand, Jesus at my left hand.
Jesus at my right foot, Jesus at my left foot.
Jesus in all my life.

David Livingstone, 19th century

Lord of all hopefulness, Lord of all joy,
Whose trust, ever child-like, no cares could destroy,
Be there at our waking, and give us, we pray,
Your bliss in our hearts, Lord, at the break of the day.

Lord of all eagerness, Lord of all faith,
Whose strong hands were skilled at the plane and the lathe,
Be there at our labors, and give us, we pray,
Your strength in our hearts, Lord, at the noon of the day.

Lord of all kindliness, Lord of all grace,
Your hands swift to welcome, your arms to embrace,
Be there at our homing, and give us, we pray,
Your love in our hearts, Lord, at the eve of the day.

Lord of all gentleness, Lord of all calm,
Whose voice is contentment, whose presence is balm,
Be there at our sleeping, and give us, we pray,
Your peace in our hearts, Lord, at the end of the day.

Jan Struther, "Lord of All Hopefulness, Lord of All Joy," 1933

Lord, Thou knowest better than I know myself that I am growing older, and will some day be old. Keep me from getting talkative, and particularly from the fatal habit of thinking that I must say something on every subject and on every occasion.

Release me from craving to straighten out everybody's affairs.

Keep my mind from the recital of endless details—give me wings to come to the point. I ask for grace enough to listen to the tales of others' pains. Help me to endure them with patience.

But seal my lips on my own aches and pains—they are increasing, and my love of rehearsing them is becoming sweeter as the years go by.

Teach me the glorious lesson that occasionally it is possible that I may be mistaken.

Keep me reasonably sweet. I do not want to be a saint—some of them are so hard to live with—but a sour old woman is one of the crowning works of the devil.

Make me thoughtful—but not moody, helpful, but not bossy. With my vast store of wisdom it seems a pity not to use it all, but thou knowest, Lord, that I want a few friends at the end.

"A Mother Superior's Prayer," Anonymous

Give me, O Lord, a steadfast heart, which no unworthy affection may drag downwards;

Give me an unconquered heart, which no tribulation can wear out;

Give me an upright heart, which no unworthy purpose may tempt aside.

Bestow upon me also, O Lord my God, understanding to know Thee, diligence to seek Thee, wisdom to find Thee, and a faithfulness that may finally embrace Thee.

St. Thomas Aquinas, 13th century

I praise Thee while my days go on;
I love Thee while my days go on;
Through dark and dearth, through fire and frost,

With emptied arms and treasure lost,
I thank Thee while my days go on.

Elizabeth Barrett Browning, 19th century

Take my life, and let it be
Consecrated, Lord, to thee;
Take my moments and my days,
Let them flow in ceaseless praise.
Take my hands, and let them move
At the impulse of thy love;
Take my feet, and let them be
Swift and beautiful for thee.

Take my voice, and let me sing
Always, only, for my King.
Take my intellect, and use
Every power as thou shalt choose.
Take my will, and make it thine;
It shall be no longer mine.
Take myself, and I will be
Ever, only, all for thee.

Frances Ridley Havergal, "Take My Life, and Let It Be," 1874

Fill us, we pray Thee, with Thy light and life,
that we may show forth Thy wondrous glory.
Grant that Thy love may so fill our lives that we
may count nothing too small to do for·Thee, noth-

ing too much to give, and nothing too hard to bear.

So teach us, Lord, to serve Thee as Thou deservest, to give and not to count the cost, to fight and not to heed the wounds, to toil and not to seek for rest, to labour and not to ask for any reward save that of knowing that we do Thy will.

St. Ignatius of Loyola, 16th century

I bind unto myself today
   The power of God to hold and lead,
His eye to watch, his might to stay,
   His ear to hearken to my need;
The wisdom of my God to teach,
   His hand to guide, his shield to ward;
The word of God to give me speech,
   His heavenly host to be my guard.

St. Patrick, 5th century

O Lord, our Christ, may we have thy mind and
   thy spirit;
make us instruments of thy peace;
where there is hatred, let us sow love;
where there is injury, pardon;
where there is discord, union;
where there is doubt, faith;

where there is despair, hope;
where there is darkness, light;
and where there is sadness, joy.
O divine Master, grant that we may not so much seek
to be consoled as to console;
to be understood, as to understand;
to be loved, as to love. . .

St. Francis of Assisi, 13th century

Notes and Bibliography

CHAPTER 1

1. Emil Brunner, *The Divine-Human Encounter*, trans. Amandus W. Loos (Philadelphia: Westminster Press, 1943), p. 66.
2. Alfred, Lord Tennyson, "Morte d'Arthur" (first pub. 1842), in *The Complete Poetical Works of Tennyson*, Cambridge ed., ed. W. J. Rolfe (Boston: Houghton Mifflin, 1898).
3. Cecil Osborne, *Prayer and You* (Waco, Tex.: Word Books, 1974), p. 69.

CHAPTER 2

1. Brother Lawrence, *The Practice of the Presence of God* (Old Tappan, N.J.: Fleming H. Revell Co., 1958).
2. David Wilkerson with John and Elizabeth Sherrill, *The Cross and the Switchblade* (New York: Pyramid Books, 1964).

CHAPTER 3

1. The Evangelical Sisters of Mary, Canaan, Darmstadt, West Germany.
2. Albert Schweitzer, trans. W. Montgomery, *The Quest of the Historical Jesus* (New York: Macmillan, 1968), p. 399.

CHAPTER 4

1. Joseph Scriven, "What a Friend We Have in Jesus," (1855), *The Baptist Hymnal* (Nashville, Convention Press, 1975), hymn 403.
2. Martin Luther, in Mary W. Tileston, *Daily Strength for Daily Needs* (New York: Grossett & Dunlap, 1884), p. 311.
3. Attributed to François de Salignac de la Mothe Fénelon (1651–1715), Archbishop of Cambrai.

CHAPTER 5

1. Spoken words of Martin Luther as related by Harry Emerson Fosdick in *The Meaning of Prayer* (New York: Association Press, 1915), p. 185.
2. Schweitzer, *The Quest of the Historical Jesus*, p. 402.
3. Fosdick, *The Meaning of Prayer*, p. 190.
4. Elizabeth Barrett Browning, *Aurora Leigh*, book 2 (New York: C. S. Francis & Co., 1857).
5. Dietrich Bonhoeffer, *The Cost of Discipleship*, trans. R. H. Fuller (New York: Macmillan, 1948), p. 42.

6. Alfred, Lord Tennyson, attrib. by Harry Emerson Fosdick in his book *The Meaning of Prayer*, p. 114.

7. Cuthbert Bardsley, Bishop of Coventry, and William Purcell, Canon of Worcester, *Him We Declare* (Waco, Tex.: Word Books, 1968).

8. Dietrich Bonhoeffer, *Letters and Papers from Prison* (New York: Macmillian, 1967), p. 189.

9. Fosdick, *The Meaning of Prayer*, p. 185.

CHAPTER 6

1. Sören Kierkegaard, *Attack upon Christendom*, trans. Walter Lowrie (Princeton, N.J.: Princeton University Press, 1944), p. 122.

2. Emil Brunner, *The Divine-Human Encounter*, p. 69.

3. Phillips Brooks, "O Little Town of Bethlehem" (1867), *The Hymnal of the Protestant Episcopal Church in the United States of America* (New York: The Church Pension Fund, 1940), hymn 21.

4. Lloyd John Ogilvie, *Cup of Wonder* (Wheaton: Tyndale House, 1976), p. 53.

5. George Meredith, *The Ordeal of Richard Feverel*, rev. ed. (New York: Charles Scribner's Sons, 1921), p. 75.

CHAPTER 7

1. William D. Longstaff, "Take Time to Be Holy," in *The Best Loved Religious Poems*, ed. James Gilchrist Lawson (Old Tappan, N.J.: Fleming H. Revell Co., 1933).

2. Richard Chenevix Trench, D.D. (1807–1886), Archbishop of Dublin, "Prayer," in *The World's Great Religious Poetry*, 1946 ed., ed. Caroline Miles Hill (New York: Macmillan, 1923).

3. Richard Monckton Milnes, "The Sayings of Rabia," sec. 4, *Palm Leaves*, 1844.

4. Richard Chenevix Trench, ibid.

5. William Shakespeare, *Hamlet*, III, 3, 1. 98.

6. Dr. Charles Farah, in *The Edge of Adventure* Response Manual by Bruce and Hazel Larson and Keith Miller (Waco, Tex.: Word, Inc., Educational Products Division, 1974).

7. Thomas Moore, "As Down in the Sunless Retreats," stanza 1, in *The Poetical Works of Thomas Moore* (New York: Worthington Co., 1887).

8. Catherine de Hueck Doherty, *Poustinia* (Notre Dame: Ave Maria Press, 1975), p. 67.

9. John Tyler Pettee, "Prayer and Potatoes," in Nathaniel K. Richardson, *One Hundred Choice Selections*, vol. 5, ed. Phineas Garrett (first pub. 1866; reprint Freeport, N.Y.: Books for Libraries Press, 1970; dist. Arno Press, Inc., New York, N.Y.).

10. Hartley Coleridge, "Prayer," in *New Poems of Hartley Coleridge*, ed. Earl Leslie Griggs (London: Oxford University Press, 1942).

11. Edwin Hatch, "Breathe on Me, Breath of God" (1878), in *The Hymnal of the Protestant Episcopal Church in the United States of America* (New York: The Church Pension Fund, 1940), hymn 375; J. G. Whittier, "Dear Lord and Father of Mankind" (1872), ibid., hymn 435.

12. Alfred, Lord Tennyson, "In Memoriam," part 32, stanza 1, in *The Poetic and Dramatic Works of Alfred Lord Tennyson,* Student's Cambridge ed., ed. W. J. Rolfe (New York: Houghton Mifflin, 1898).
13. Jane Cross Simpson, "Prayer," in *Bartlett's Familiar Quotations,* 12th ed. (Boston: Little, Brown & Co., 1951).

CHAPTER 8

The Confessions of St. Augustine. Translated by the Rev. E. B. Pusey. New York: E. P. Dutton, Everyman's Library Edition.

Enlarged Songs of Praise. London: The Oxford University Press.

Goudge, Elizabeth. *A Diary of Prayer.* New York: Coward-McCann, Inc., 1966.

Hymnal of the Protestant Episcopal Church in the United States of America, The. New York: The Church Pension Fund, 1940.

Masterpieces of Religious Verse. Edited by James Dalton Morrison. New York and London: Harper and Brothers, Publishers, 1948.

Tileston, Mary Wilder. *Daily Strength for Daily Needs.* New York: Grosset and Dunlap, 1884, 1901, 1912, 1928.

Uncommon Prayers. Collected by Cecil Hunt; American edition arranged by John Wallace Suter. Greenwich: The Seabury Press, 1955.

World's Great Religious Poetry, The, 1946 edition. Edited by Carolyn Miles Hill. New York: The Macmillan Co., 1923.